OUT OF THE SHADOWS

REESE BLACK

ISBN: 978-1-7348098-0-0

Many thanks to Troy Black, Larissa Runyan, Caleb Jones, and Christa Cicardo for making this book better.

TABLE OF
CONTENTS

Introduction....................................7

Chapter 1.....................................17

Chapter 2....................................35

Chapter 3....................................57

Chapter 4....................................95

Chapter 5...................................115

Introduction

For some reason I never read book introductions as a kid, but please read this one.

I love to cry. I'm not your typical, emotional movie sobber. (Although I do cry when I watch *The Lord of the Rings*, and when I read *The Lord of the Rings*, and when I think about *The Lord of the Rings*.) I don't look for sappy stuff to cry about, but I love to cry over particularly happy or bittersweet moments. I cry when I drive away from my family in Texas to return to where I live in Oklahoma, because in a world where many have nowhere to call home, I am blessed to have two. I cry when I give speeches at weddings, because if there is any time you can unabashedly describe your love for a friend in front of a crowd, it is at a wedding. Plus, people give you a lot of compliments on your speech afterwards if you shed a few tears. I cry when I see other people crying, because honestly, I just don't want them to hog all of the fun. You may think all of this crying threatens my image as a manly, masculine man. Fortunately for me, I have the face and body of a twelve-year-old baby boy, so no one is startled much when I burst my eye-dams in public.

My favorite time to cry by far, however, is when I am spending time with God. There is something so potent about my heavenly father's love that when I feel him[1] close, my eyes want to pour out enough liquid to fill a hundred bottles of trademarked Holy Tears for me to sell on TBN. These emotional outbursts get me into awkward situations from time to time, but I don't mind them. In fact, I can remain completely unaware of the awkward situations I create.

———

My first Sunday at college, I am driving with two previously unknown people to a previously unknown church. Less than an hour after meeting my new friends, I break down in tears right next to them during praise and worship. Soon after, I cheerily walk and chat with them back to the car, extolling the service we just enjoyed—oblivious to my friends' concerning glances to each other. On the drive back, they build up the courage to ask if I am okay.

"I'm fine!" I say.

"You were crying during service," says the driver, delicately.

"Oh, that? I do that all the time!" I say.

Feeling it necessary to account for my tears, I delve into a lengthy monologue about all that God has done for me. I tell them how I grew up in church, how I fell into depression and

---

1 Having grown up in a Christian tradition that reverentially capitalizes all pronouns referring to God, I feel the need to explain my decision to refrain from that practice in this book. For me, the decision is entirely aesthetic—I simply like the way it looks to have all pronouns uniformly lowercase. Considering that the reverential capitalization of pronouns did not become popular in the English language until the nineteenth century, and that several modern translations of the Bible refrain from reverential capitalization, I didn't feel the need to utilize the practice in this book. Although, I respect anyone's decision to use it in their own writing.

suicidal thoughts at the age of fourteen, how I felt my strong morals and self-righteousness utterly fail me, how I got trapped in a cycle of sin and self-hatred, and how Jesus—the God I thought I knew everything about—showed up one night, spoke to me, saved me, and changed me.

I am now bawling in the back seat of the car. My new friends shift uncomfortably in the front seats and let out an occasional cough. Later, once we know each other better, my friends explain to me why this was awkward for them. I had no idea, of course. Social minutiae tend to pass over my head when I'm hunched over with my face in my hands.

—

Since that time, God has added many more wonderful things to my list of stuff to cry about, but none do I cherish more than the closer relationship I have with him. A wise man recently told me, "As soon as you put God in a box, he will show you the box." I have found this to be true. I can hold assumptions about God for years. They serve as walls for me to organize my Christian life within. Over time, I hear God tapping on the sides of the walls, until I finally realize that he is outside of them. God never forces me to give up my assumptions. He points out how wrong they are. He lets me decide what I want to hold on to: the box or him.

Lately, I've been thinking a lot about myself and God and the Church[2]. Specifically, I've been thinking about myself and God and the Church in relation to where I live—Oklahoma City, Oklahoma. If you haven't been to OKC, then you haven't

---

2 Speaking of capitalization… When I write "Church" I am referring to all Christians together being the body of Christ in the world. I'm distinguishing it from "church" which I use to describe a building, organization, or event that is created by members of the Church.

truly lived. At least, you haven't lived in OKC I mean. It's a quirky place—a bizarre mashup of city and country. It's a city whose boundaries are so expansive, you can get completely lost driving across open planes while still technically being in city limits. It's a city where you can slurp down a delicious bowl of pho, prepared by the children of Vietnamese refugees who immigrated here in the 60s, while smelling Okie barbecue roasting in the restaurant next door. Fry up some Southern hospitality, add equal parts hipster and cowboy, toss in an excessive number of colleges, garnish with uniquely identifiable surrounding towns, sprinkle with minor earthquakes and devastating tornadoes to taste, and you're ready to wash down a steaming bite of Oklahoma City with a glass of sweet tea.

What I've been thinking about lately concerns the churches. In OKC, we have every kind of church you can imagine, all on the same street—and the street next to it, and the street next to that street. If you took an aerial view picture of the OKC metro and wanted to mark every church with a pen, you could save time by dipping the photo in a jar of ink as long as you're fine with a two percent margin of error. We are the buckle of the Bible Belt. And I love it. As a Christian, it's nice to live in a place where Christianity is the norm.

However, when I look out across this city I live in, I can't help but think that we as the Church of OKC are missing something. With a concentration of Christians as dense as this—our city should be a model of heaven. We should be driving godly renewal into every realm of society, and our city and state should feel the impact of this. Instead, our city and state are racked with problems. At the time of writing this book, Oklahoma has the highest incarceration rate in the world. As a state, we rank near the bottom in the country for many areas that determine quality of life, such as education, mental health, and even physical health. In OKC, there are whole sections of our community that seem forgotten by the Church at large. I see many neighborhoods stricken with poverty in a city where steeples mark every street corner. I see many homeless, sick, or hopeless in a town full of the disciples of Jesus.

What ever happened to the power and impact of the earliest Christian Church—the drive and ability to flip the world upside down with the love of God? I see too little of this, not just in my city, but across the Western Church as a whole. We are called to be a city on a hill. But rather than moving powerfully in places of business, government, education, and all other facets of our society—to care for others and reveal God's love to the world—it looks like we are sitting in the background. Why isn't the Church making ripples throughout all of society? Why does it feel like the Church is hiding—keeping its head down instead of jumping into the action?

Before I continue, let me say that this book is not really about how churches or individual Christians need to be doing more to impact the world. Personally, I do want to see more churches focus their efforts on solving specific problems in their cities. I want to see more Christians restructuring society within every sphere of influence available to us, including the arts, government, and business. However, there are already a lot of inspirational messages out there about how the Church should be doing more to change the world. This book focuses on a different subject. I want to speak to a deeper, underlying issue that helps explain why the Church has taken a backseat in our society instead of grabbing the steering wheel and determining its destination. Having clarified this, I can now introduce the main point of this book.

The reason the modern Church is hampered in affecting the world in powerful ways is because it is hiding from the kingdom of God. The Church, individually and corporately, is hiding in the shadows, far away from the light of heaven.

I know this may sound like a crazy assertion. We as Christians love God and want to be closer to him. How then can we desire to be closer to God and also shrink from him and his kingdom simultaneously? In order to explain this, I'm going to need to turn into a Lego.

Imagine a large, flat Lego piece. This Lego is me. (The Lego piece is green by the way; green is my favorite color). You'll notice that the Lego piece has straight rows of uniform bumps. These bumps represent everything about what makes me, me—the way I was raised, the way I think, my values, my emotional dynamic, my personality, etc. Now say there is a pile of small plastic pieces nearby. These plastic pieces represent new ideas about God, the Church, and me. Now imagine someone tries building a tower by stacking these plastic pieces on top of the me-Lego piece. As pieces are placed on top of me, one of two things is going to happen. If the plastic piece in question is shaped like a Lego, it's going to attach to me. If it isn't shaped like a Lego, it won't stick to me. You could say that my properties as a Lego determine the kind of tower that can be built on me, and that any builder who wanted to construct a non-Lego tower on me would be out of luck.

Now imagine that an artist comes along. He sees my Lego-self and the pile of plastic pieces, and he decides to construct a masterpiece sculpture on top of me. Except, he doesn't want to use any of the pieces in their original form, so he starts to use fire to melt them down and shape them into new pieces that fit together in new ways. To build on top of me, he's going to have to reshape me with fire, too. As a Lego piece, this fire petrifies me. It's blindingly bright and unbearably hot. I'm too scared to even think about what the artist is trying to do. All I know is that if I get too close to the fire, I am going to melt—I'll lose all my rows of small bumps that make me, me.

As Christians, we love to engage in Christian disciplines. We hit up churches like they are places to pick up free puppies. We read the Bible like candy is stuffed in the pages. We pray like this week's winning lottery number is written on the inside of our eyelids. We do these things a lot. Even if you don't think you do these things enough, if you are a Christian, it's likely you do them more than non-Christians do.

Although we're trying to pursue God through spiritual disciplines, we can still run into the issue of the Lego. I may want God to do something new in my life, but if I'm as rigid as a Lego block, nothing truly new can be built on me. The substance of my deep, inner-self determines what I receive. Jesus illustrates this truth with his parable about the sower and the different soils. My soil determines what God can grow in my life. If I'm not willing to let God change the depths of who I am, then nothing about my life is going to change, no matter how passionately I engage in spiritual disciplines.

—

This afternoon, my brother Troy calls me from Texas while I'm making popcorn.

"What are you up to, bud?"

"I'm just making popcorn."

I don't own a popcorn popper, so I always make my popcorn on the stovetop. My brother tells me about a P.G. Wodehouse novel he finished reading last night. As he talks, I hold the phone in my left hand and use my right to pour oil in the bottom of the pot, turn up the heat, and dump in the kernels.

"I just started writing a book," I say.

I watch a hundred golden eggs explode into edible clouds as I try and explain my ideas about God and the Church that I want to write about. Around the time I run out of words, my right hand is dumping cayenne pepper all over the tiny edible clouds.

"I think I know what you are trying to say," my brother starts.

I'm listening, but I'm also thinking about the time I brought my spicy popcorn to a party. A girl thought she was having an allergic reaction to it because she didn't know it was supposed to be spicy; she couldn't figure out why her tongue was burning.

"It's like that verse about drinking milk when God desires for us to be eating meat by now.[3] I think a lot of Christians hear that verse or are challenged in some way and then try and do better. But their reaction is, 'I've got to start drinking a lot more milk,' or 'I need to find a way to drink milk way faster.'"

My right hand is scooping up the red speckled clouds with a large spoon and dumping them into my mouth.

"Yeah. Yeah, that's good," I gurgle through a mouthful of allergenic-free, spicy popcorn.

—

As Christians, it's common for us to hide from the fullness of God's kingdom at least in some areas of our lives. Let me be clear: I'm not talking about salvation. When I believed in Jesus to receive salvation, God opened up the door for me to come into his kingdom. However, it's entirely up to me how far into that kingdom I want to journey. If I want to hang out at the outskirts, experiencing as little of God's rule and authority in my life as possible, I'm more than welcome to. But if I want to walk closely with God, that will require discovering what he's like—discovering what living in his kingdom is truly meant to look like.

Being unlike God is what keeps us far from God, and we can be unlike God in many ways. We can think differently than he does. We can feel differently than he does. There are many traps of fear, emotional wounds, bitterness, doubt, and unhealthy beliefs about God, ourselves, and the Church that can ensnare us—keeping our minds and hearts far from the mind

---

3 Hebrews 5:11-14

and heart of God. I see these traps as large pits along our journey into the center of God's kingdom, the center of what he is like. I believe Satan digs these pits for Christians to fall into. The body of Christ is falling into them all the time, and as a result, our spiritual growth is stunted.

However, it is not so simple to define these issues as just covered holes that we accidentally fall into from time to time because the enemy wants our destruction. There comes a point when we have resided in one of these pits for so long, despite the multiple ladders of escape that are available to us through the truths presented in the Bible and across Christian tradition, that we are no longer living in a trap or prison but—very bluntly—a hiding hole. Even a hole, when lived in long enough, will begin to feel like home to us. Once we become comfortable, any external attempt to free us from our lengthy trapped state will not look like deliverance but instead a forced eviction. It's an eviction from what we use to make sense of the world, make sense of God, and make sense of ourselves. Our reaction will instinctively be to run from the source that is trying to draw us out, or possibly even to attack it.

This is why I say the Church is hiding from God's kingdom. We've built mental and emotional constructions—ways of living and interacting with our faith. But these constructions are based largely on religious notions, tradition, personal experience, and even unresolved emotional suffering. These constructions can leave us toiling in religious activity without actually taking a single step closer to God. In order to draw us into him, God is working to dismantle our constructions so that he himself can be the bedrock of our lives. Allowing God to do this is ultimately satisfying. But the process? It's confusing, frustrating, uncomfortable, and sometimes even terrifying. It's much easier to put up barriers, maintaining distance from God at all times. It's safer to stay away from the fire and therefore the prospect of melting. But there's a reason God calls us into the process.

At the end of it, we find who we were always meant to be. We find what the Church was always meant to be. And finally, we are empowered to transform the world into what it was always meant to be.

This book is my story. It's also the story of what God is doing in the Christian Church today. It's a story about finding healing from emotional wounds and unhealthy beliefs. It's a story about going on an authentic pursuit of who Jesus really is. It's a story about walking out of the shadows—out of the traps of the kingdom of darkness—and stepping fully into the light of God's kingdom.

Throughout this book, I'll address some of the pits we can fall into and decide to live in. Before you continue reading, though, I need you to do me a favor. I need you to relax. Try not to let yourself think that you need to work harder to get out of these pits and be a better Christian. The problem with the Church isn't a lack of work but a lack of accepting God's work. I believe God has built all of us ladders to climb out of our hiding holes so we can move closer to him. My goal is to help you find one of these ladders he's made for you. I'm not trying to inspire you to claw your way out. That being said, the pit is dark, and I don't know which wall your ladder is leaning against. It might take some searching around in order to find it. Let's look for it together.

Chapter 1

In which I realize I am at the age where I get invited to so many weddings.

I have a best friend—his name is Caleb. There are numerous things I like about Caleb, but one of my favorites is his eccentric taste for adventure. One time, Caleb moved to Costa Rica. Knowing Caleb, I knew there was a good chance he'd end up getting married to a Costa Rican girl, have twelve kids, and build a bed and breakfast on the beach, so I made it a point to say my goodbyes before he left. But Caleb didn't end up getting married in Costa Rica. He was actually there for school, and he is an extremely serious student. The semester he spent there, he was entirely dedicated to his studies. So dedicated in fact, he barely had enough time to start dating one of his American classmates. Joy is a girl with a fitting name. In Costa Rica, she broke both her wrists in a bike crash and still had a better attitude about it than when my tea gets cold before I finish drinking it. After Costa Rica, Caleb moved to Texas to be close to Joy. One morning, Caleb went to her house and woke her up before the sunrise.

"Caleb? What? What's going on?" she asked, wrapped in a blanket with her eyes half open.

"Wake up! Come on! It's going to be a great day! We're going to go watch the sunrise!" Caleb said, nervous, and all smiles.

"What time is it?" She asked. Her alarm clock blinked some unholy hour made only for rolling over in bed.

Caleb had a place in mind, a park with a perfect view of the horizon. He drove there with Joy yawning in the passenger seat.

In Texas, the sun is old and crotchety. If you're outside around two in the afternoon, you can hear his bitter rays yelling at you to get off his brown, baked lawn. But, in the earliest of the morning, before the sun is fully visible, he thinks of his youth and some sweet star he loved before she moved to a different galaxy. Caleb and Joy caught this side of him, all teary-eyed and sentimental. Before long, he saw the couple watching him, hugging for warmth amidst the cool morning dew. Soon, he got jealous and resorted to his old cranky self.

After the sunrise, Caleb and Joy cooked breakfast together, a Costa Rican dish they almost lived on, and then they started off to do a list of things Caleb had planned for the day. There were places all over town he wanted to go: an aviation museum, a certain coffee shop, and a lakeside for a picnic and an acoustic guitar worship session. He had a theme running through their destinations and activities. They were all the things that had helped bring them together. Joy was understandably curious about Caleb's insistence to do and see so many things in one day, but she followed along without knowing what was really going on. Until, she arrived at the last destination.

With interlaced fingers, they strolled through a park to where trees and bushes grew in a ring. They followed a path of flower petals and candles into a decorated grove. Caleb put down his backpack, pressed play on his phone, and soft music filled their grassy dance floor. As they danced, Joy began to cry. Through tears, she spotted the heads and feet of friends and family unsuccessfully hiding behind bushes. Then, Caleb proposed. She said yes. The whole world emerged at once to rejoice with them.

Here's what I love most about this story: Joy didn't have any idea of what Caleb had in mind when he woke her up too early. To her, it was just another ordinary day, like so many other ordinary days. But for Caleb, this was one of the most important days of his life. He wanted to make Joy happy; he wanted to express his deep love for her. He had all these exciting plans to bring her delight. Even though she didn't know any of this, even though she had no idea where they would end up at the end of the day, she still got to experience all of it. All she had to do was get out of bed.

> Arise, my love, my beautiful one,
> And come away,
> For behold, the winter is past;
> The rain is over and gone.
> The flowers appear on the earth,
> The time of singing has come,
> And the voice of the turtledove
> Is heard in our land.
> The fig tree ripens its figs,
> And the vines are in blossom;
> They give forth fragrance.
> Arise, my love, my beautiful one,
> And come away.[1]

---

1 Song of Solomon 2:11-13 TPT

I can divide my life into three parts. The first is the period when I grew up in a Christian home, regularly attended church, and did not know Jesus. The second began after Jesus saved me from an internal hell. The ecstasy of him lifting a mountain of shame from my heart sent me running and shouting from the church camp auditorium where I received sweet salvation. Three and a half years later, I transitioned into the third period of my life. It began with the first of two questions—two questions that would change my life forever.

"If you moved away today, and never saw anyone from college again, who would you miss?"

Jason has a knack for asking questions—good questions, hard questions. If there was a reward for most meaningful conversations started, it'd be hanging on Jason's wall. He and I have been roommates for a couple months, and I feel like he knows me better than people I've known for years. He's a senior and I'm a freshman, still in my first semester of college. This is my first time living away from my parents, so Jason's taken it upon himself to be my guide into adulthood. He's been actively coaching me in all areas of life—even how to dress. ("Are you wearing a navy blue shirt with navy blue pants with navy blue shoes?" "Yeah. Is there something wrong with that?")

I first met him when I visited the college as a senior in high school. It was a preview weekend for high-schoolers, and I spent a couple of days living in the dorms. My room was basically a cardboard box with a window cut out, just large enough to fit a bicycle and a twin mattress. It connected to a living room, which connected to two other cardboard box sized bedrooms, a bathroom, and one bedroom larger than the others. Two more high school students were crashing on the living room couches. The other bedrooms housed the college students who actually lived there. The larger bedroom belonged to Jason.

Jason rapidly gained my respect. He could sing, he could dance, and he could beat any living person in a Super Smash Bros. match on the Nintendo 64—the triple threat to my friend auditions. My first night at the dorm, a half dozen guys and I cheered around a TV screen as we button mashed our way to outdated-video-game-console glory. Jason's skills were unmatched. A high school kid with something to prove, I channeled every ounce of my mental dexterity into my tri-pronged, plastic controller just to be a competitor. I was so focused, I didn't even notice when a noxious fume began emanating from the bathroom. Jason did. He slipped away for a few minutes to tell a couple of dudes in the dorm below us to stop smoking the pot that was currently wafting up the air vents. Then he came right back and killed us all in another round of Smash. I thought he was the coolest. The next year, Jason requested me as a roommate. Now I live in my very own cardboard box, with a living room connecting me to Jason, our third roommate Travis, and our makeshift kitchen.

I think about Jason's question for a few moments. Since I arrived at this Christian university, I've heard a lot of talk about community—about finding a group of friends to "do life with." People tell me that the relationships I am building now will be the ones that will last me the rest of my life. I think about the friends I've made here. The people I spend most of my time with when I'm not studying, the people I've stayed up late talking to, the people I've driven around with to explore the city—each of them cross my mind as potential candidates for miss-ability. If anyone else on campus asked me the same question, I would have answered by listing these friends. But Jason asked me the question, and I trust Jason.

"Jason, I wouldn't miss anyone here if I never saw them again. I mean, maybe you, a little, but missing people isn't something that I do. I don't think I've ever really missed anyone except for my family."

The words come out casually, devoid of emotion. I must have always known this abstractly; I just had never formed the thought before. How else could a statement like this fall out of my mouth before I knew what I was saying? My answer takes Jason aback. I see his countenance bending to express the level of concentration he maintains in each of our serious conversations.

"Why do you think that is?"

"I don't know."

I think hard about the friends I've had over my life, and my mind goes way back—back to when I was a child.

"I didn't really connect to a lot of kids my age growing up. I was homeschooled, and I lived in the country. I was in baseball and 4-H and stuff, but I was super close to my siblings, so I didn't really need other friends. Four of my siblings were older than me, so kids my age seemed kind of immature and I didn't get along with them very well. In seventh grade, I started going to the small, Christian private school most of my older siblings graduated from. There were a few guys in my class I became pretty close friends with. But my parents had to take my sister and I out because of money stuff, so my freshman year I started going to a regular public school…"

I stop. My drive down memory lane has been going smoothly up to this point, but suddenly it feels like I hit a pothole. A past scene starts playing in my head. I see a gold colored minivan pull up to the back of an aged high school building. The passenger door swings open. Out steps a thirteen-year-old boy carrying a black trumpet case; on the side, a blue strip of tape displays the name "Reese" in black permanent marker. He stands still for a few moments at the edge of the concrete courtyard before him. Walls of red brick and arched windows line the perimeter. On the left wall, an assorted group of students holding an assorted collection of black plastic cases huddle close to an open door. Instrument squeaks sound from the door to mingle with the group's chatter. The thirteen-year-old boy shuffles his feet toward the noise. With each step, his tennis shoes smear the courtyard with a doubtful residue, marking his path from the golden minivan to the band hall. I see the line stretching out behind him, and in it, I can read his thoughts: "I don't know how long I'm going to be here. It might only be a year or two. I can't get too close to anyone; I don't know how long I will be here."

The memory dissipates. I'm back in my dorm living room. Jason waits for me to continue. When the conversation started, he was tidying up the room—straightening the coffee table and lamp, smoothing out the rug and blinds. Jason keeps our living room clean and well decorated. Other guys from our hall call it the Oasis. They come in from time to time to escape the desert of their messy dorms by sitting on our vacuumed couch covers. At the moment of my epiphany, the cleaning has stopped. Jason and I are standing in the middle of the room, and I am yelling.

"Jason! There's something wrong with me! I don't let myself get too close to others, cause I'm afraid one of us is going to leave! I did it all through high school! I thought I was going to switch schools again after a year, but then after a few years at the same school, I realized we were all going to graduate soon and go our separate ways. Now I'm in college, and the first thing I thought when I got here was that I can't get too close to the people here because I'm going to be gone in four years. Holy crap! If four years isn't enough time for me to build a close friendship with someone, how much time do I think I need?!"

I'm fired up now. It feels like English class. When I decipher any symbolism from the assigned reading, I tend to shout out my interpretation in excitement. This time, however, I've been studying the text for years, and my answer is full of as much anger as energy.

After our conversation, I begin to wonder about the friendships I've had. Did my old friends miss me, even though I didn't miss them? Have I ever had a close relationship, besides the ones I was born with? Can I become close friends with someone—what would that even look like? I don't know how to proceed. The reveal of this issue shakes my heart, but nothing changes. I decide to do the one thing I can—what I often do when I'm out of ideas. I pray. I begin to ask God to send me a friend. Not just any friend, but a friend who can teach me how to be someone who misses his friends. In between my prayers, I start up an abysmally attended swing dance club in the university's creepy basement, I get a job calling high school kids to tell them how awesome college is, I do a lot of homework, and after most of the semester passes, I take my first trip back to my home in Texas.

"I feel like God wants you to forgive your father," the church elder tells me.

I'm visiting a church near my home in Texas. It's a fairly charismatic church, one of those churches where complete strangers feel no hesitation when walking up to you to say, "God wants you to forgive your father." It's been a while since I've attended a church service. I still haven't found a church I like back in Oklahoma City. It's strange. I've attended a church my entire life, whichever one my parents happened to be going to. Now I'm realizing how hard it is to shop for a new church in a new town, and how easy it is to sleep in on Sunday. I like this church, though. It's a bit more serious than I'm used to, almost frighteningly serious, but I feel God's presence and see a lot of meaningful praying occurring. I like it, and I feel ready to go along with anything.

"Okay," I say.

And I start praying, telling God that I forgive my dad. I forgive my dad…but for what? I've got a pretty great dad. I can't think of anything to forgive him for. Nevertheless, I forgive you, Dad—for whatever it is.

Right before the end of the semester, a few weeks before the next question—the second of the two questions that will change my life—something else of consequence happens. I break down.

Jason steps into our living room singing. That man never has a bad day, I swear. I lie prostrate on the couch, my face buried in an exceptionally clean cushion. When the song comes to a close, Jason asks:

"How are you doing, Reese? Are you tired?"

"Jason, I'm a failure," I moan into the cushion. I'm usually a good deal more positive than this.

"What?"

I turn my head.

"I'm a failure." Having delivered, in my opinion, a more than satisfactory answer to his inquiry, I return to my incomprehensible moaning.

"What are you talking about?"

To be honest, it's a bit difficult to explain. I've had a decent week. My first semester of college ends in a handful of days. My grades are fine; I've made no disastrous blunders since arriving here; I haven't gained a pound towards the freshman fifteen (the trick is to avoid the dessert line in the cafeteria). Absence of supporting evidence affects not my conclusion: I am a failure. I know it intuitively. I try to put words to my crisis.

"When I graduated high school, I had all these ideas of what I wanted to do in college. I wanted to start a club; I wanted to practice the piano and banjo and start writing my own music; I wanted to find a church and start volunteering there; I wanted to meet a city manager and see if I could get an internship working for city hall. I haven't done anything. I've tried starting a swing dance club, and I've had maybe five people show up to my dance classes all semester. I haven't learned a single song. I visited four churches, I didn't like any of them—I haven't even been to a church up here now in two months. I haven't met anyone who works for a city government. I've been here an entire semester, and it feels like everything I've tried to do has failed. I have less of an idea now of what I want to do after college than when I graduated high school. I feel useless."

My dry monologue leaves me emotionally empty. I stop acknowledging Jason. I've said what I've said, and I don't care what he thinks, or what he has to say about it. Nothing is going to change my mind or the way I feel about myself. Usually I'm consumed by social niceties; my ninth grade year, no one knew I was struggling with depression, not even my family. I hate being a downer. Today though, I have no energy left for appearances. I can't make eye contact with the world anymore or even nod politely to her trite observations. My newly improved disposition: bitter dejection.

After a moment of silence, Jason speaks. His words come slowly—testing the ground before he commits to a verbal path.

"I don't think you're a failure. From everything I've seen, you're doing well at your first semester of college. I see you balancing your school, work, and your relationships. You're involved in several clubs here, and I hear people talk about you. They say that you do a great job at everything you're a part of, that you add a lot to the university."

Jason's encouragement comes to a close. Although he is thoughtful and sincere, I feel no better. There can be nothing left to say, I think, so I suppose I will be left to my moping. But after some more silence he says:

"I'm going to put on some music and spend some time worshiping God."

And he does. Right there in the living room, he hits play on his favorite worship album, lifts his hands, and begins to praise God. I roll off the couch and take three steps to our shared bathroom. In a moment, I return to sit upright on the couch; the music drowns out the sound of the toilet running. Jason prays, sitting on our second couch. I'm sucking in deep breaths, letting them out slowly, trying to feel better. I listen to Jason's exaltations of God. I listen to the portable speaker as it sings praises to God from the coffee table. The room becomes church, and I miss church. Since the day I met Jesus, three and a half years before this moment, praise and worship has been my favorite part of organized evangelical gatherings. It occurs at the beginning of the service of most churches I've attended—lots of people singing and praying, telling Jesus how great he is, how thankful they are for what he has done for them. Something about it feels so right to me. I almost get mad when the preacher stands up and starts yapping, cutting off the worship time. I can lose myself in worship to Jesus, cause I know he's done something great for me. Maybe not today. Maybe I don't feel like he has done anything for me today, but I know he did something good, even if it was three and a half years ago. I already feel a little bit better.

Jason stands up, walks across the room, and sits down right next to me. Our combined weight compresses the exceptionally clean couch cushions, causing us to lean into each other's shoulders. The music plays on while Jason speaks.

"While I was praying, I felt like God wanted me to tell you something for him."

And then he says:

"I love you."

And he says it again.

"I love you."

And as I sit, leaning into his shoulder, listening to these words, I'm taken back to that moment—three and a half years ago.

It was the summer after my freshman year of high school. I was fifteen. I had been struggling with depression and suicidal thoughts for nearly a year. The Christian morals I was raised in had failed me, but I was still attending church and trying my best to act like a good Christian without any troubles. I was fake, I was hurting, and I hated myself.

Here's how it started. When I switched from a private Christian school to a public school, I knew I would be exposed to a lot more ungodly behavior than I was used to. I knew I had been fairly sheltered, and I knew I would be startled interacting with kids that cussed, had sex, drank, or did drugs. But I also thought I could walk the halls with those kids and come out unchanged and unscathed by immoral influences. I thought I was the perfect example of Christian morality. More than that, morality was my identity. I was a good kid. A good kid was who I was, who I had always been. Going to a school with bad kids was a chance to show off how much better than them I was. In short, I was prideful. I thought I was miles above the average teenager.

At first it worked. A couple weeks into public school life, I prided myself at how my behavior stood out among my peers. I was already known as the good kid there, the kid who had never gotten in trouble and never done anything wrong. But a change started to occur. Slowly, I began to taste the sickly sweet waters of sin. I had no idea how close I was to drowning in it. This is what broke me: it didn't come from any outside negative influences. It wasn't the kid in marching band telling me how great smoking pot is. It wasn't the kid in Spanish class bragging about his sexual experiences. It came from inside my own heart. Lust was growing from within me. The very vice I condemned—heard condemned my entire life from the pulpit and read condemned from the Bible—I was entertaining it. I began fantasizing about having sex. It started a little at a time, but soon it filled every idle moment. The habit changed me. It changed how I viewed women, but more than that, it changed how I viewed myself. Before, I thought I was impervious to sin because of how disciplined I was in monitoring my physical actions. I never looked at porn, not once. I never slept with anyone. And yet, here I was, willingly engaging in what Jesus calls, "adultery in the heart." I was a walking, talking pile of guilt.

I tried to push it away, the guilt and the habit. I pretended that I didn't have a problem; I pretended that I wasn't starting to hate myself. I learned to pretend, and I became the facade of a kind, well-behaved human. I went to church, and every Sunday I would repent, quietly to myself. I would ask God for forgiveness, and I promised to try harder to kick my habit. *Vanity.* I went to school, and every day the self I projected and the self I knew grew further apart. *Grasping for the wind.* The guilt turned to self-hatred, and the self-hatred turned my mind to thoughts of death. I know it sounds dramatic, but this was the state I was in. Life felt like an unbearably long string of pointless, painful days. I wake up, I try, I fail, I feel guilty, and I repeat again and again and again for sixty-five-plus years. *So I hated life, because what was done under the sun was grievous to me.* Nothing helped. When I tried to be righteous—praying, reading the Bible, and avoiding sin—I felt shameful. When I tried to abandon my sense of right and wrong—tossing morality aside and acting as I please—I felt empty. *I hated all my toil in which I toil under the sun.* I was worthless, a literal bag of worm food waiting to be devoured.

Like I said, it was the summer after my freshman year of high school. One of the first things I did that summer was attend a weeklong, Christian summer camp out in the piney woods of East Texas. The morning of the first day, a few other teenagers from my church and I meet our camp counselor, a Newfoundland native in his mid-twenties named Andrew. I have no idea how Andrew found his way from a Canadian island to the Lone Star State, but here he was, dialing back his accent so we could understand him. He had short blonde hair, an athletic build, and exuberant mannerisms. Everything he did or said was excitement and smiles. My group tried our best to keep up with him as he ran from the slip-n-slide to the soccer fields to the climbing wall and back around again. Between activities, he wedged in lots of questions to get to know us, and also laughed out insane stories of escapades with friends both in Texas and Newfoundland. He also told us stories of things he used to do frequently before he knew Jesus. Things like drinking six too many stouts and picking drunken fights outside of bars. Without changing his lighthearted tone, he would follow up these types of stories with raw confessions of the pain and emptiness that plagued his psyche for most of his life. Getting wasted and fighting was a means of escape, for a moment, from the ever looming meaninglessness of his own existence. I had never once gotten drunk. The scraps I had been in were so mild that Elmo wouldn't classify them as fights. But with that feeling—the emptiness—I related.

Andrew's stories splashed into my stagnant pool of a heart and made small ripples of hope. It was his transparency that struck me. He wasn't being polite or saving face. He wasn't fake. He was himself, fully, without a mask. As we interacted, my own mask sat heavy on my face. After months of hiding my pain, my personality was nothing more than a skillfully-crafted facade. We juxtaposed terribly. I felt like I was masquerading at a party, conversing nervously behind my Thalia while all other attendees chatted in normal attire. Compared to Andrew, I was a habitual liar. The circular track of misery I was driving was becoming unbearably predictable. I desperately needed a different road to turn down, or at the very least some speed bumps.

As I looked through this clear glass pane named Andrew, I saw something different: joy. Joy poured from his being and enveloped him—an aura thick with palpable waves of freedom and satisfaction. Even while talking of past sorrow and destructive habits, Andrew's countenance shown with contentment. His past misery paralleled my current. He said meeting Jesus changed his life. I can't tell you how many times I had heard stories of Jesus renewing someone's life. I can't tell you how many times I asked Jesus to renew my life that past year to no effect. Seeing Andrew though, I could see the work of Jesus with my own eyes. I realized then that I had been asking God for help out of dim hope. I hadn't ever believed that he actually could help me, or even wanted to help me. Seeing Andrew, I believed for the first time that God truly wanted to help.

That night, all the campers attended a worship service followed by a sermon. The speaker talked about sin that becomes habit, sin that we fall into again and again even if we are trying not to. He talked about the way it feeds on our soul, taking more and more from us. He talked about how sin promises freedom and enjoyment, but in the end turns us into its slave. I have no idea how anyone else received the message that night, but I felt like the speaker was talking directly to me. The sermon pulled firmly on my strand of memories. I followed the strand to the beginning of my freshman year, and I could see clearly my transformation into an ouroboros—the moment I was first tempted to bite my own tail. My insides turned throughout the message. At its close, the speaker invited all to the front of the auditorium to pray with their counselor. I'm not sure I would have gotten out of my seat. Moving one inch toward the stage equaled admitting my issues to other people—something I had never been capable of. But suddenly, before I could consider the invitation, I heard a voice. Except, the word "heard" doesn't accurately describe what I experienced. A step closer: I felt a voice. It came from inside. Beginning in my chest cavity, the voice echoed through my body in reverberating sensations. But still, I understood the words clearly—as clear as a whisper in my ear.

If you go up there right now, you'll never have to deal with this again.

The voice I heard—never had I heard it before. I believed it to be God. He was making me a promise. There was no way to verify the source of the voice, nor guarantee its promise. But the voice had an almost physical effect on me, like a small hand pushing me forward. I couldn't imagine what would happen if I stood up, but I knew nothing would change if I stayed sitting. Like I said before, I was desperate for change. So, I stood. I walked the aisle. I found Andrew. I told him. I told the first person—speaking slowly in concise words—about the sin I could not free myself from. Then we prayed together. I asked Jesus for help. And as Andrew prayed for me, something happened.

What I noticed first was similar to this: you're standing in a room when suddenly an industrial sized fan shuts off and all falls silent; you look around perplexed—you were accustomed to the noise and never noticed the fan had been running. The noise I now noticed as missing was a voice and a gnawing. The voice had been internal, and like the voice with a promise, I had been feeling it echo in my body. But this voice had been quiet and dark. It had whispered these words for an evil span of time: "You are worthless." I had never heard the words clearly, but now in their sudden absence, I remembered them punctuating the misery of my year. The gnawing too had ceased. It had been a slow and tortuous pain in my gut, like some biting worm had been feeding upon my intestines. I could feel that gnawing now only in memory. I gasped. Without these noises, everything felt new. Each knot of tissue, each flutter of emotion, each spark of a neuron. My attention expanded, engulfing all aspects of my being simultaneously. All felt fresh and unmarred as my mental finger stroked body and soul. It was like being thrown from a pool of acid into a pool of clean water. The shock of it; I was in awe.

Then the second change took place. It felt like a bead of air lodged itself deep in my chest. It inflated rapidly, expanding into a large, firm bubble. My chest felt enlarged, and I inhaled deeply to fill the growing space in my lungs. With the bubble came a pleasurable feeling of lightness. The balloon in my chest was pure helium, and my feet almost came off the ground.

Then came the total eclipse. The voice. The voice from before. The voice that made me a promise. It sounded from within my chest like a gong, reverberating throughout my entirety.

You are worthy. You are worthy because I love you.

The words filled my soul as a fire hose fills a kiddie pool. I cried. Loudly. As I bent over, my tears formed two streams, arching away from my eyes, joining under my nose, sweeping up a flow of snot, and cascading off my lips—a waterfall of facial fluids splashing on the concrete between my feet.

Several minutes passed, and I left the pool of tears behind me to return to my camp group. They were sitting quietly, watching reverently as kids received prayer at the front of the room. I tried telling them what just happened to me. I began urging them, if they had any sin or pain they wanted to be free from, to walk up to the front and have Andrew pray for them. They didn't stir or speak, but looked at me with compassion, or possibly concern. I then realized I had been crying as I talked to them. It was too difficult to explain; I removed myself to sit for a while in my overwhelming feelings.

When I finally left the auditorium, I walked in solitary darkness along the path to my cabin. With the boughs of the piney woods rising above me to block all man-made lights, I tilted my head back to see brilliant sparkles of stars. As I gazed upward at countless specks of blazing beauty, the earth receded from me. I stood lightyears away from all, a celestial body in some heavenly orbit. I alone existed, the only human ever created, and around me swirled the Spirit of God and the stars. I burned from within—freedom and joy rose up like flames in my body. I yelled and I ran and I danced. I danced under the stars.

As I lay down to sleep, in a large wooden cabin with dozens of teenagers, my eyes stayed wide open. My mind mesmerized me. The old pattern, the familiar walk through a perverted and sickly imagination that always led to greater levels of self-hatred and depression was gone. I stared into blackness. My thoughts wandered. I did not fear where they would go, for each path lead back to the place these words had been engraved:

You are worthy. You are worthy because I love you. My eyes watered again. Slowly, I drifted from consciousness, carried along by the flow of these words. *You are worthy because I love you. Because I love you. I love you.*

"I love you," Jason says a third time.

And suddenly, it doesn't matter why I thought I was a failure. I had somehow allowed myself to believe I was worthless again. But I know now, my worth isn't determined by how well I do at anything. I'm worthy because Jesus loves me.

Something breaks inside me. My feelings of failure leak out of some internal vessel, and the love of God pours in from above. I lay my face down on Jason's lap and begin to cry. Loudly. There's a growing dark spot on his pant leg where my tears and snot gather. He hugs me the best he can considering the awkward sitting position we've found ourselves in. After some time, our roommate Travis comes in and stands in bewilderment at my emotional spectacle. A few moments later, he fetches me a box of tissues and sits on the opposite couch in reverence. I continue to weep. And the semester ends. And I return to Texas for Christmas. And I continue to pray for a friend that can teach me what it means to be a friend. And I never expect the next question—the sudden arrival of the second question that would end up changing my life.

Chapter 2

In which I learn that Oklahoma wind is ludicrous.

It's the first day of my second semester of college. The Christian university I attend requires all students to take four ministry classes regardless of major. I'm sitting in one of these four classes: Biblical Life and Ministry. I'm hyped for this class. I've always been both an academic nerd and a Bible nerd. For me, a college Bible class is a beautiful intersection of nerdiness. Plus, I've heard promising descriptions of our professor.

"He's brilliant," they said.

"His class changed my life," someone told me.

"He's a crazed, ancient philosopher bent on destroying all hope and beauty on earth with time-bending lectures, incomprehensible tests, and compulsive throat clearing," declared a few others.

The consensus is that he's eccentric, and eccentricity is enough for me to love a person. Our ancient philosopher takes the podium. My college is fairly laid back, and most professors spend the first day covering the syllabus and little else. (Or if the class is small enough, they have everyone introduce and talk about themselves. I know—it's a very small college.)

Our philosopher stands for no such mincing of time. He says he wants us to get our money's worth out of his class. Although, I think perhaps it is his gray hair spurring him on, a constant reminder that his days are numbered. After rushing through the syllabus, he immediately commences his first lecture. He begins with a question.

"What does it mean to have a relationship with God?"

He waits in silence for an answer. The question lingers in the mind of thirty freshmen. What he is asking about is the most basic tenant of Christianity. The work of the cross—what Jesus accomplished on earth—paving a road between humans and the divine. The majority of the class considers themselves Christians. If you asked them if they have a relationship with God, most would answer with an unwavering yes. Ditto for me. But no one answers this question, and the silence grows awkwardly long as the philosopher paces, scanning the audience for a response. I imagine there must be a number of things a person could say. None of them come to me at the moment, nor to my peers apparently. Or maybe we're scared—scared to give a wrong answer to an intimidating professor on the very first day of class. He answers it himself.

"Well." He speaks slowly, overly enunciating for the benefit of our underdeveloped brains. "When you have a relationship with a person—that means that you talk to that person, and that person talks back to you."

I'm struck. This is the simplest, almost juvenile, answer to the question possible. The lecture continues, but the answer remains in my mind. It's disturbing. Why should such a simple answer bother me? After pondering it for most of the class, the crux finally hits me: I only have half of the equation.

I talk to God every day. My prayers extend back further than I remember—one continuous monologue of gratitude and requests directed toward heaven. It began in my early childhood when my parents taught me to pray. Now in adulthood, the monologue continues daily with religious fervor. But does God talk to me?

I think about what I hear believers say about God's voice. Some say God talks to us through the Bible. Verses will "jump off the page" and that is how God speaks to us today. I've experienced something like this before. Although, it's extremely infrequent. Others say God speaks to us through other people, especially other believers. Again, I believe this has happened to me, probably a few times, and most recently with Jason. It seems odd, though, that God would primarily convey his messages to the wrong person with the hope that he or she will deliver it to the intended party. I imagine a mailman who intentionally puts letters in the wrong mailboxes just so he can watch people run around the neighborhood trying to straighten everything out. Some say God talks to us in mysterious ways, like through songs on the radio or the shapes of clouds or unlikely coincidences. And, I have felt like God was trying to tell me something before in some mysterious way. But, it was always frustratingly unclear. Also, when I read the Bible, I see very little of this kind of communication occurring. I think about Abraham, Moses, Paul, and so many others. When God had something to say to them, it looks like he just said it.

A minority of believers I've met say God speaks to them clearly and directly. This happened to me, once, at that summer camp. I'm immensely grateful for the words he spoke to me and for the freedom and joy he planted in my heart. Yet, I can't help but think how strange a friendship is where one speaks incessantly and the other says only twenty-two words over the entire duration of the relationship.

Days pass, and I'm still absorbed by the question and answer. I think about it in chapel. Twice a week, the entire campus meets in the university chapel to sing songs and listen to a short sermon. I look around at hundreds of open mouths, forming the vowels and consonants of "hallelujah" in slow motion. Does God speak to them? What about the people on stage, the musicians and the guest speaker. Do they hear from God? My ears develop a sensitivity to the subject. I overhear a classmate, one I know to be full of Christian zeal, say that God told him to break up with his girlfriend. I'm surprised by this, considering that only last semester he said that God told him that he should date the girl in question. Does God change his mind about who he's shipping?

It's a Christian campus, and like me, a lot of my peers are concerned about whether they are following the plan God has for them. We all want to do what God wants us to do. But, hardly anyone I know has a firm grasp on what that is for them. It's like we all believe God wants to speak to us, to tell us what to do with our lives, and none of us are hearing from him. Except boyfriend-of-the-year, of course.

I'm naturally an emotional person. My heart is a steam engine, and dilemmas have a way of clogging valves, building internal pressure till the whole system is on the verge of exploding. Once the pressure increases, certain menial tasks can become nearly impossible for me to perform. In this case, those menial tasks are what many refer to as "spiritual disciplines." You know, stuff like reading the Bible, going to church, and praying—only the most basic Christian practices—nothing too important. I try to keep up these practices, as I have my entire life. But God isn't speaking to me through them. I've always believed I have a relationship with God. But if he isn't speaking to me, if I'm only spiritually monologging, then maybe I don't.

I pick up my Bible, and I try reading a little bit of the gospels. Every word I see I've seen before. Each scripture I've read and heard countless sermons on. I'm on my way to memorizing the Bible, and it reads like lifeless bombast—like The Pledge of Allegiance recited by high school freshman in second period computer class. The pressure builds. Trying to remain calm, I place my Bible back on my desk. I lay on my bed and try to pray.

"My Father who art in heaven…thank you God for…I ask that you…in this difficult season…please bless my…help me to hear…in the name of Jesus."

My intercession sounds like so many religious phrases to be repeated again and again and again before a deaf idol. And there is no response. Whether speaking or resting in referent silence, I hear no answer. I'm conversing with a wall. Anger rises in my chest. I slide off my bed, and while struggling to slow my breathing, I tie my shoes and head out of my dorm for a run. I try not to think about it. And each day I repeat this, and the pressure builds.

I'm lying in bed. It's past midnight, and I can't sleep. My mind won't leave this subject alone, and my chest buzzes with emotional activity. In high school, I heard a lot of talk about young Christians who stop going to church and ultimately give up their faith during their time in college. I never thought I could be in danger of becoming one of those young people that make their pastors weep. I don't want to give up my faith. If anything, my soul is desperately grasping for faith. But I don't feel like myself. I've spent four and a half months now in OKC, and I still haven't found a church. I sleep in on Sundays, only to wake up to a fresh plate of guilt. I wish I could find a church I enjoy, but the thought of visiting another holy building makes my stomach lurch. I can't sit through another religious ritual. I'm already required to attend chapel—where the seats are full but the service is empty. My once fruitful quiet time has all but dried up. Today, a successful Bible study session is one where I drop my Bible after five minutes of frustration rather than hurl it across the room. Like I said, I don't feel like myself.

I jump out of bed, throw open my closet, and start pulling on layers of clothes. It's mid-January. I know the cold will be bitter. I climb back up onto my bed and grasp the bottom of my dorm window with both hands. It slides up slowly, till my curtains shake violently in the night air. I've been climbing out of my first floor bedroom window for months. I've only used it for fun—a mildly exciting backdoor. Now, I honestly don't want to risk my roommates hearing me pass through the living room and front door. I don't want anyone asking me why I decided to take a late night walk through the chill of winter.

I slide through the portal and land in the dark. Immediately, a freezing gale punches the bare skin of my face. I turn toward the brick wall and pull on my hood. The icy wind slingshots around the dormitory, piercing my jeans. For a moment, I consider climbing back into my bedroom. I step up on a gas gage, grab the top of my window pane, and pull it shut. I turn and run through the night. The campus is minuscule. In moments, I'm past the last building and heading out far into an empty field that borders the university. I run to the edge of a wood. I slow my pace. I look back. A handful of buildings glow in the distance. I look up. A handful of stars twinkle in the abyss.

A comfortable distance from sleeping ears, I yell. This is why I'm here: to scream profanities at the night sky. I shout. I curse. I barrage all creation and the God who made it with a list of expletives. Could this be some kind of therapy? I'm running out of four letter words. I transition to more comprehensible accusations.

"Why won't you say anything!? It doesn't matter if I pray or go to church; you're like a brick wall! I thought I had a relationship with you, and now I don't even know what that means! I don't know what this is supposed to look like, and I just get angry when I try to talk to you!"

The cold wind catches my words and carries them west. They never reach heaven. My shouts released some pressure from my chest at least. I listen to the silence for a few more moments. I begin shivering. I jog back toward campus.

In the next two weeks, I repeat this two more times. Yelling at God is the closest thing to prayer I do anymore. This isn't new for me. The first time I yelled at God in the middle of the night, out in some lonely place, was during my freshman year of high school. When I was struggling with sin and depression, a few months before I met Andrew, I raged at God one night—blaming him for creating me to live such an awful, meaningless life. After Jesus saved me, I still went out and yelled at God a few more times throughout high school. But, I only yelled at God for one reason: girls. I needed some way to vent my relationship frustrations, and I've always had a compulsion for the dramatic.

I thought I would be over this by now, though. I was saved, right? And I'm not some heartbroken high schooler anymore. I shouldn't need this. I know this is a terrible response to God. But, it's also the only thing that makes me feel better.

I'm wearing a mask again, although it's thinner than four years ago. This mask doesn't try and tell others how great of a Christian I am. It just says I'm doing okay. I'm not going to tell a friend what's happening to me—that isn't an option. If I told a friend, I'm sure they would invite me to church or something. They've already invited me to their churches. I visited them. I'm not going back. There is one friend, though—one friend who has yet to invite me to church.

"Hey Reese, are you doing anything Sunday night?"

I'm reading in the living room. I haven't really talked with Jason for some time. He works several jobs, is training to be a financial advisor once he graduates in a few months, and he's planning an elaborate proposal for his girlfriend who runs an orphanage in South Africa. He's a busy guy.

"No, I've got nothing going on. What's up?"

He tells me about how he met this guy at the coffee shop he works at. His name's Grant, and he and his wife started a church in their home recently. Very recently. In fact, this Sunday night is the first time for them to hold a worship and prayer service in their living room.

"You should come this Sunday. I think you would really like it."

I respect Jason. And I do wish I had I church I could go to without getting angry.

"Okay. Yeah, I'll check it out."

Sunday night, I drive to the address Jason gave me. It's in an unassuming house in a typical middle-class neighborhood. I'm a little nervous. I've never met these people, and now I'm pulling up to their house at dusk. Jason will be in there, but I have no idea who else will, or what this house church will be like. I stop my car in front of the mailbox.

It's moments like these, when I'm faced with the unknown and uncomfortable, that a part of me says to pivot-turn back to safety. I've listened countless times before, and in certain cases, I think for the best. But if there is one thing I've learned, it's that I don't want to spend my life hiding inside a giant pillow fort. Stepping beyond my comfort zone forces me to grow. That's why I've made it a habit to say "yes" as often as I can to unfamiliar opportunities, especially ones that give me butterflies. It's about becoming a better person—or it at least makes for some good stories. This is what I tell myself to get me out of the car. I walk up to the front door and knock.

"Hi! Nice to meet you! Glad you're here!"

Grant is a tall, energetic man. We exchange pleasantries as we walk into the living room, and I'm immediately caught up with the noise and activity. There are six more adults in mid-conversation, almost as many kids playing on the floor, and a Christian album sounds through the TV above the fireplace. Jason gives me a hug. I shake hands with the rest. So far, I'm loving this. My college is extremely small, and I have no other friend groups in the city. Being somewhere new, talking to someone new—it's a welcomed change. Grant looks around like he's about to make an announcement.

"Alright! We are going to get started!"

The scene changes rapidly. Bodies whirl about. Two adults carry and lead the kids out of the living room, disappearing upstairs. Hands drop glasses of water on coasters and pick up musical instruments. The living room settles, and the transformation is complete. The social gathering from before somersaulted and stuck the landing as a jam session. Sitting or standing along the far living room wall, every person is now fingering a piano, guitar, microphone, or box-drum. Every person—except me.

Guitar in hand, Grant sweeps the living room quickly with his eyes. I am standing alone in the middle of the living room, a few feet away from the praise band. I am the congregation. Grant looks at me and coughs out a short, uncomfortable chuckle. I can tell he must think this is awkward for me. He addresses the assembly of one.

"Well, we're gonna play some songs and just spend time worshiping God. Don't feel like you have to stand here in the living room; you can go anywhere in the whole house if you want to sit and pray or do anything that you want."

I nod to Grant. I'm glad he said as much. The vibe from these musicians says, "Hey, no pressure. This isn't a performance." There's no churchy pretense in this—just some friends worshiping the Lord together. Plus, Grant grossly overestimated my ability to recognize awkward moments. I feel fine right here, facing the band. I'm not going anywhere. They start the first song. Then something happens.

Seconds into the music, I feel something ignite around me. I sense movement, and an energy fills the room, like heat radiating off a fire. Birds flying free in the kitchen; dust storm swirling through the hall; mudslide slushing down the stairs. A vacuum forms, sucking all air from the house through the windows, pumping it back in, and sucking it out again. The presence of God is here.

My entire life, I have loved worship in church because

that was where I most strongly felt the presence of God. But I believe that God takes his presence away from me when I'm not acting the way he wants. If I'm not killing it as a Christian, God's presence leaves me—I won't feel his love again until I do at least a week's worth of disciplined spiritual practices. And I've never failed at being a Christian like I have this year. I don't go to church, haven't for a semester. I get nothing out of chapel. I haven't prayed or read my Bible for nearly a month. And on top of this, I'm angry. Angry at God for not speaking to me—I know this must be a sin.

Yet, his presence engulfs me. I'm bewildered. I should not be feeling this. Guilt is what I deserve. And God's love holds me like a hug.

I burst into tears. I fall forward. I lay sobbing on the ground, two feet from the worship band. He glances down at me sympathetically—uncomfortably—and tries to return his focus to worship. And Grant thought worship was going to make *me* feel awkward. I reversed the awkwardness and shot it right back at him. On the floor, silently, I pray.

"Why? Why do I feel your presence after this month? I'm doing everything wrong. How can you love me like this right now?" I ask him almost harshly, like I'm upset he broke some kind of rule.

I leave that night perplexed. And nothing changes. I try to pray and read my Bible a few times with the same results as before. All of my spiritual effort leaves me frustrated and empty. The week passes. It's Sunday night again, and I drive to Grant's house once more. I'm propelled here. I have to know: after another week failing as a Christian, will I still feel God's presence during worship?

I do. Except this time, I take Grant's suggestion from last week. I go find a place to sit. I'm crying in the hall now, with my butt on the floor and my back against the wall. I'm also not the only congregant. Several more adults are here, worshiping or praying, spread out across the living and dining rooms. I feel his presence as strong as before. I'm as befuddled as before.

Sometime after worship finishes, the small church gathers loosely in the living room to pray. After some corporate prayer, we break off into handfuls to pray for one another. A man who wasn't here last week addresses me. As best as I can tell, he's a thirty-something poet—sporting a golf cap and plenty of facial hair. He has a determined look on his face, and he gets straight to the point.

"I feel like God wants you to know something. I hear him saying that he wants to be your father, and he wants you to be his son."

The first thing that comes to my mind is the question. That one annoying question. The question that's been plaguing me all month. "What does it mean to have a relationship with God?" I know what he is saying is true, biblically. When I entered into Christ, I became a son of God. I know he's technically my father. It's even in the Lord's Prayer: "Our Father in heaven…"[1] But I also know my sonship doesn't seem very real. Me saying, "God is my father," parallels me saying, "I have a relationship with God." The pivotal words—father and relationship—have only ethereal meaning, not substantive meaning. But my experience tonight, and last Sunday, cut a line through my religious expectations of what interacting with God is like. A part of my heart swells with hope. It knows what the poet says is true, truer than the ways I've known it before. I nod to the poet and say nothing.

"I feel like something needs to happen here. God wants to impart his love as your father to you. I think it would be a good idea, if you're comfortable, for you to give Bob a hug. Bob's sort of representative of an older, fatherly figure. I think giving him a hug will help you receive God as your father."

The Bob in question is standing next to me. He's an elderly

---

1 Matthew 6:9 ESV

man with a white mustache. He's got a sturdy frame and hands coarse from years of manual labor. He reminds me of my grandpa. I look at Bob. His eyes are already starting to get watery.

"Okay," I say.

I give Bob a hug.

Holding onto a complete stranger, I hear a voice reverberating inside me.

You're my son. I see you as my son, and I want to be your dad. I love you, and I want to be your dad.

The words penetrate my heart. It's more than words—it's an answer. What does it mean to have a relationship with God? He's my dad, and I'm his son. This isn't a transfer of knowledge; my brain already knew this. This is an adoption process.

I've got a good earthly dad, but God is not like my dad. He is more loving and understanding in every way. The weight and reality of being adopted by a perfect father sinks into my soul. My heart is screaming, "I belong! I'm somebody! I'm not alone; I'm not unwanted! I'm God's son!" The validation smothers me.

I'm crying, of course. Tears drop one by one onto Bob's shoulder. I hold on tight. It's God's arms I feel around me, not Bob's. My religious view of God shatters in this moment. He wasn't withdrawing his presence from me. He wasn't waiting for me to start being a better Christian before he decided to speak to me. God wanted to be close to me, but he didn't force his way in. Like with my friends throughout my life, I wasn't letting him get close.

After some time, I let go of Bob. The evening ends. Over the next several weeks, I think, I pray, and I return to the house church each Sunday night. I notice a shift has taken place inside me. Something was resolved the night I hugged Bob, and I begin to understand exactly what it was. That man at that highly charismatic church in Texas I visited in the fall—his words come back to me.

"I feel like God wants you to forgive your father."

Since I was a young boy, I didn't feel good enough, smart enough, strong enough, whatever enough—I've always been insecure in who I am. I wanted someone to tell me I'm valuable. I looked to my earthly dad to do this for me. My dad did tell me he loved me. He did compliment me from time to time. But he didn't fulfill that need. Most of the time, I felt like my dad thought I was incapable—a failure. I developed a strong desire to impress him. Somewhere inside, I thought if I could perform well enough—morally, athletically, academically—then he in return would give me the sense of validation I needed. But no matter how hard I tried, I never felt like I did enough. Whatever love or validation I wanted from him, I wasn't capable of earning it.

It seems almost universal that the way a person views their father shapes the way he or she views God. If our dad is unkind, God must be unkind. If our dad is absent, God must be absent. Just as I had been acting to impress my father, I also was trying to earn God's love. That's why I broke down on Jason's lap last semester. That's why I struggled with feeling like a failure. My whole Christian walk, I tried to perform well enough in hopes that God would be pleased with me, all while firmly believing I should be doing more, I should be performing better. Performance was who I was, and shame was my clothing.

This is why I kept God at a distance. I couldn't let myself be close to him when in my heart I believed he was disappointed with me. For this perceived disappointment, I was even angry with God, as well as with my dad. This is what I need to forgive my earthly father for.

Dad, I forgive you for not validating me as a capable and valuable person. I recognize that what I wanted from you is something that men cannot give, but rather, it is freely given by God when we become his children. And when summer comes, I'll tell you "I forgive you" in person.

February could not be more different than January. I go to a church I love. I stop running around outside at night and yelling at things. I enjoy chapel. I stop wanting to throw my Bible across my room. The most dramatic change, however, is in my prayers. I stop rehearsing my religious monologue. Now when I pray, I sit in silence for a few moments. Then I say one word.

"Dad."

And I feel him close to me. I sit there in silence, dumbstruck by his love. And if I do at some point start saying more words, I call him "Dad" the whole time I'm praying. I didn't consciously make this change; it just sort of happened.

Beauty unfolds as the semester rolls on. Life no longer feels like a competition I'm always losing at. I'm learning, and I love learning. A portion of this learning occurs in my classes. But most of it happens in my dorm room while talking about God with Jason, in the offices of professors while talking about careers, around a ping-pong table while talking with students about theology, and in the laundry room while remaining dead silent because the girl I think is cute is doing her laundry right next to me and I'm too nervous to say anything.

Most of the rest of the learning occurs at the house church. I've never seen any ministry like it. The pastors, Grant and Rachel, felt strongly that God wanted them to start a church in OKC. They moved their family here and prayed about the church for a year before having people meet at their house for prayer and worship. With a history in ministry, they purposely threw out everything they ever learned about how to start a successful church, and they relied on the Holy Spirit to tell them what he wants their church to be like. As such, they have a unique church strategy. As far as I can tell, it consists of pretty much one thing: ask God to show up. They believe when we worship God, when we invite the Holy Spirit to come, that he shows up and does incredible things. Their expectation is palpable.

At the moment, our Sunday night services are almost entirely worship and prayer. Everyone spreads out across the house to worship God while the band plays. Some sing, some sit and pray, some lay on the floor, some jump around, and one lady wails. Each of them unashamedly pour out their hearts in adoration to God, and the Holy Spirit comes like I've never experienced him before. Most worship services I've been to felt like singing songs in the general direction of heaven and hoping God could hear them. Here, God's in the room.

When worship finishes, we meet in the living room to pray. I'm used to prayer circles—people taking turns praying for the church, people in the room, or whatever happens to be on their mind. That's part of our prayer time. The rest is foreign to me. I'm not used to a group of people sitting in silence, waiting for the Holy Spirit to tell them what to pray for. I'm not used to people praying intentionally over one another based on what they feel like God is saying. In short, I'm not used to what occurred the night I hugged Bob, and that kind of thing happens all the time here. I'm no longer attending church just to listen to a preacher. I'm engaging with God and ministering to others. I'm a part of the ministry team—we all are. This stirs up my heart to know God more. Since the time I was saved to today, Jesus has never been more real to me. Since the time I was born to today, I've never been more excited to be alive.

Newness abounds, save one area. One aspect of last semester did bleed into this one. I still pray for a friend—a friend who can teach me how to be a friend, a friend who can teach me to miss people. I'm a part of my church in a way I've never felt a part of something before. However, I'm not deeply connected to any one person there.

Jason talks about his best friend, Robert, every now and then. He once told me about Robert's wedding. Jason was the best man, of course, and he gave a speech about how Robert helped him grow as a person. He talked about all the ways his life had changed for the better because of their friendship, and Jason's valuing of Robert was sincere.

If someone asked me to be their best man, I'd feel like a total poser. Even if someone valued me enough to ask, I can't imagine valuing them in that way. If I ever give a best man speech, anything beyond "so-and-so is a cool guy" will feel insincere for me. That meaningful friendship Jason talks about, I have no idea what that would be like. It's always just been God and I versus the world. I'm social, but my heart's a loner.

So I continue to pray. The recent shift in my relationship with God gives me hope. I'm no longer so afraid to let God be close to me. Maybe that means I can let a friend closer too.

Jason casually mentors a lot of students who live on campus. I'm used to interrupting these mentorship sessions on a regular basis. I swing open our dorm door and walk right into a serious discussion between Jason and another student. I quickly slip into my room and shut the door, and they jump back into a personal conversation about relationships, spirituality, life, etc. Lately, there's been one student who's conversations I've been interrupting a lot. He's a skinny, dirty-blonde haired guy who's a couple years older than me. His short, gruff facial hair and propensity for smiling says, "I've been camping in the woods for three days, and I'm really happy about it!" A few times now, I've barged into the dorm room just as Jason and him finished their serious discussion, so I stuck around and talked instead of rushing to my room. Before now, I've interacted with Caleb quite a few times. I've seen him around campus, and he's even good friends with my other roommate. I always thought he seemed like a pretty cool guy. By catching the tail end of his and Jason's conversations, I learn why he started coming over to our dorm so often.

Caleb grew up as a pastor's kid. He's always been involved

in ministry, whether working at church camps or leading worship. When he began interacting with Jason, though, he started to feel like he was missing some aspect of God. Jason told him about the time he tore a ligament in his knee playing basketball. A group of Christians prayed for his knee, and it was miraculously healed. Jason's doctor was flabbergasted by the near instant recovery. Jason told Caleb about his relationship with the Holy Spirit. The Holy Spirit speaks to Jason and often gives him encouraging words to tell others or shows him ways to pray for people. This was all new for Caleb. It challenged his beliefs about God immensely. Caleb didn't back away from this challenge though. It made him hungry. This ravenous hunger for more of God, Caleb and I share.

I'm still surprised, though, when after he finishes talking to Jason in his room, he comes into my room and starts talking with me. He's starting to come into my room a lot now. Even when Jason is at work, Caleb walks right into our dorm, knocks on my door, and starts talking with me. I don't know what to do. I've never made an effort to hang out with Caleb. I've never even been in his dorm room. Yet, here he comes, over and over again to ask me about me how classes are going, what I want to do when I graduate, about my relationship with Jesus, and about my experience growing up in church.

One day, Caleb walks into my room and says:

"I really want to go hiking in the Ouachita National Forest this Saturday. It's in South-East Oklahoma. Do you want to come?"

I throw my backpack—recently emptied of school books and filled with hiking junk—into the back of Caleb's car, and we head off into the rising sun. The plan is simple: four hours of driving, four hours of hiking, and four hours of driving again. The thought occurs to me that I've committed the next twelve hours to hanging out exclusively with Caleb, and honestly I'm a bit nervous.

"We don't really know each other that well," I think. "What if we run out of stuff to talk about and are forced to sit in uncomfortable silence for half the drive."

Luckily, Caleb downloaded several episodes of the NPR radio show, *Wait Wait...Don't Tell Me!*, so the trip starts easily with laughter and an explanation from Caleb for my question, "What exactly is a podcast?"

Things are going well. Then Caleb and I realize that we're both hungry and didn't pack nearly enough energy bars for the whole day. We'll stop somewhere for an early lunch, we agree, and then stop for dinner on our way back to campus.

As chance would have it, we hit a festival at the next small town we drive into. The old, downtown street is lined with booths, and Caleb slows the car to a crawl as groups of people cross the street on their way to festivities. We look up to read a large banner strung above us. "Annual Frog Leg Festival." Caleb's and my excitement rises to an unhealthy level.

"A FROG LEG FESTIVAL! HECK YEAH!" we both yell.

He parks immediately, and we head off down one side of the street to look for food and small town oddities. A surplus of homemade items sell on every corner. Surprisingly though, the festival has an appalling lack of frog legs. We can't find them anywhere. We spot two restaurants farther down the street, and we decide it would be best to eat a substantial meal and get back on the road. The farther establishment is a Mexican food place, but before we reach it, we have to pass the Internet Cafe. I peek through the windows and turn to Caleb.

"Hey Caleb! This place looks weird!"

That's good enough for him. We walk in with expectations high. The Internet Cafe looks like the living room of an eccentric, country grandma who hoards computers from the 90s as a hobby. License plates and homemade jewelry hang from the walls, and outdated monitors, clunky computer towers, and white dollies cover the half dozen mismatched tables and chairs.

On our way to the counter, we squeeze past an elderly gentleman checking his email. A middle-aged woman takes our order: two steak burgers. Caleb and I find the one surface in the shop not cluttered with monitors—a small table with a checkerboard.

After beating Caleb a couple of times at checkers, I look in the direction of the counter, hoping to see our meal coming toward us. I can see the small kitchen on the other side of the counter. It's empty.

"Caleb, is anyone making our food right now?"

Caleb looks up from the checkerboard.

"It doesn't look like anyone is in the kitchen."

"Where's the lady who took our order?" I ask.

"She left. She walked past us a while ago and went out the front."

I didn't notice her leave.

"Then who's supposed to be making our food?" I ask.

We both stare into the kitchen from our seats. There's no sign of movement.

"Do you see an oven back there?"

Caleb stands up and walks over to the counter to get a better look. He comes back to his seat.

"There doesn't seem to be an oven. There's a microwave."

At this moment, the lady from before swings open the front door of the shop, walks quickly past us, and resumes her post behind the counter. She starts moving around in the kitchen, hopefully making our lunch. Caleb leans close to me.

"Have you noticed no one else here is eating?"

I look around. The small shop holds a handful of senior citizens, all typing away on computers. There's no food in sight. I laugh a little.

"Oh man, I hope they're not waiting for their food, too."

I look back towards the kitchen. Our chef has placed a couple of buns on plates. This is promising, I think. Perhaps our food will be done before the next annual frog leg festival.

Then, she pulls the lettuce out of the fridge. Her motions are painstakingly slow. After each small movement, she freezes for a solid minute, as if meditating on what to do next. I watch her stack the lettuce on the buns. One. Single. Leaf. At. A. Time. Five minutes pass, and two short stacks of lettuce now sleep on their gluten beds. After finishing this task, she quickly walks around the counter again, passes Caleb and I, and heads out the shop a second time.

One game of checkers later, I'm considering hopping over the counter and finishing our unoccupied sandwiches myself. Then she returns and heads back behind the counter. For the next several minutes, we listen to our patties baking in the microwave. Finally, the deed is done. She carries out the master-pieces and sets them before us.

"Sorry guys. I don't work here."

And with those few cryptic words, she walks out of the shop, never to be seen again. We look at the food, we look at each other, we look out the glass door of the shop, and we look at each other again. I'm the first to speak.

"What do you think she meant by, 'I don't work here?'"

"I have no idea."

"If she doesn't work here, why was she behind the counter? Why did she take our order and make our food? Do you think she just walked in off the street and decided to pretend like she works here?"

We laugh, nervously. We look back down at our food.

"Do you think it's safe to eat," Caleb asks. "We're not going to get food poisoning are we?"

"Um. No. Probably not. I hope not. I'm really hungry."

"Let's pray over it, before we eat."

And with that—forty minutes after we ordered—we pray an extremely sincere blessing over our food, bite into the worst burgers we've ever eaten, and head back to the car. For the rest of the day, I have the most egregious gas.

Four hours in the Ouachita National Forest fly by. We hike through hilly woods, looking for trails and getting lost. When we finally make our way back to the car, we still have plenty of energy, so we drop our backpacks and take a two-mile trail run around a small lake at the park's entrance. Pulling out of the park, I can't stop smiling. I'm exhausted, and my shoes are soaked from crossing rivers, but this was the most fun I've had in a long time. I lean my seat all the way back, and Caleb puts on another episode of *Wait Wait...Don't Tell Me!* A few hours into driving, I'm starving and completely out of hiking food. The next town on the map happens to be home to my favorite frog leg festival.

The signs of the festival have mostly been cleared away when Caleb pulls into a spot in front of the Mexican restaurant. As we walk up the steps, I spot the Internet Cafe down the street and shudder. The host shows us to our seats. Before our waiter arrives, I turn to Caleb.

"If that lady from the Internet Cafe is our waiter, I'm leaving."

Caleb laughs, and looks around to make sure she's nowhere to be seen. When our meal does come, promptly too, it's the best tasting Mexican food we've ever had.

As the semester passes, Caleb and I continue to hang out. We go on runs. We play Super Smash Bros. with Jason. Caleb starts going to the house church. We talk about Jesus and the gifts of the Holy Spirit. Caleb decides to run for president of our college's student body government, and he asks me to be his vice-president. We make a campaign video, mainly consisting of us dancing to techno music. We win by two votes. We decide to be roommates next school year. The semester ends, and Jason graduates. I return to Texas for a few months.

My sophomore year kicks off, and Caleb and I jump head-first into running the student government. We spend nearly all our free-time trying to resurrect a club that hasn't done anything in years. We take breaks to brew tea and play video games. This is how I find myself, a few weeks into the school year, sitting with Caleb on our living room couch, sipping a steaming mug of green tea. This is when it hits me. If I left tomorrow, and never saw anyone from my college again, I would miss someone. I would miss Caleb.

"Caleb." He turns to me, sipping on his own mug. "You have no way of knowing this, but two semesters ago, I was talking with Jason, and I realized I've never had a best friend before. I realized that, I didn't know what it meant to really be friends with someone. I was afraid of letting people get close."

My eyes start to water.

"After that conversation, I started asking God to send me a friend. To send me someone who could teach me how to be a friend. Caleb, you're…"

I choke on my words, and tears fall into my lap.

"You're the answer to my prayer. I've never had a friend like you before. I feel like I understand God better because of you. It's always just been me and God—I've never been connected to someone I felt like I was growing with. But God wants us to be connected to others. He made us to experience him with others."

Tears are streaming down Caleb's cheeks.

"Reese," he tells me. "You're my best friend. We're always going to be friends."

We put down the tea and hug it out.

Two years later, I'm standing in front of a wedding party, giving a best man speech. I talk about how my friend changed my life for the better, and my words are sincere. I finish the speech in tears. On the way back to my seat, Caleb stands up and gives me a hug.

Chapter 3

In which I write about destiny while trying to avoid clichés.

My journey toward the center of the kingdom of heaven is marked by the moments God propels me out of pitfalls. In some cases, the pitfalls are religious—faulty beliefs about God and his nature, about the relationship he wants to have with me, and about the new nature he's given me. Other times they are traps of the soul—sinful behavior or thoughts, deep emotional hurts, unforgiveness, fear, and lies stemming from the demonic. On many occasions, God's work opposes a mixture of both categories. Sometimes I feel as though Jesus is pulling me out of darkness. Other times I feel as though he is pulling darkness out of me. And I know with confidence that I am walking daily into the light and out of the shadows.

The work of the Holy Spirit comes in lessons, love, and challenges. Whenever they sink a little further into my mind and heart, my whole life feels renewed. In the introduction, I wrote about how uncomfortable it can feel when the Holy Spirit tries to change us. It is uncomfortable—and immensely satisfying. When we allow him to define us more closely to the way he sees us, then our hearts are plunged into a deep, meaningful pleasure that is honestly more exciting than anything I've ever experienced. My aim is to embrace his work fully. My goal is to encourage the Church to this aim.

One of the main reasons we as Christians get stuck and are unable to move further into the kingdom of God is because we have defined God rather than letting him define himself. Growing up in the church, I had lots of ideas about who God is. I meshed doctrinal teaching and my experience in churches to form an image of God in my mind, and then I claimed to know God. For me to have said I had a relationship with God would be similar to me saying:

"I've got a girlfriend named Lucy who lives in Canada. I've never seen her or communicated with her. But I know her because people have told me about her, and so I can picture her in my mind."

It's easy for us, as Christians, to buy into the idea of salvation, since all we have to do is pray and ask Jesus to forgive us. But after this, we don't seem to know how to grow into mature and capable Christians, emulating the apostles of the early Church. We're at a loss for real spiritual growth, and for good reason. We don't know where we are going. We are trying to get closer to God, but the God we know, if defined by us, can't be sought out because he doesn't exist. When God spoke to me, telling me that he wanted to be my father, he was defining himself to me. Since that day, God has been consistently tearing away my mental constructions of who he is and what he does. He's replacing them with definitions pulled from the entire revelation of Scripture. Furthermore, he's replacing them with definitions steeped in experience.

Experience with God is key in coming to a clearer understanding of who he is and who we are to him. I daresay, for the majority of the Church, most of what we have experienced in our lives has had very little to do with God, and therefore, we know very little about him. What's worse, many Christians take their negative life experiences and use them to construct a faulty view of God. This is due to a widespread, erroneous teaching in the Church on the will of God and his sovereignty. Many teach that virtually everything that happens to us, good and bad, is a direct result of God's will. If we get sick, or if something bad happens to us, it must be part of God's will, they would say. He must have a reason for it—probably to make us better Christians somehow. The issue I have with this teaching is simple: it's unbiblical.

When Jesus' disciples asked him how to pray, he told them as such:

"Our Father in heaven, hallowed be your name. Your kingdom come, your will be done, on earth as it is in heaven."[1]

Why would Jesus tell his disciples—this includes us—to pray that the Father's kingdom would come to earth, that his will would be done on earth? For the simple reason that his kingdom isn't here now. His will isn't being done now.

"But he's God," some might say. "Doesn't whatever God wants to happen just happen?"

Anyone who thinks that way is completing discounting the will of humans and the will of Satan. As illustrated with Adam and Eve, God gave humans enormous power to shape the universe through freedom of choice. Satan also has a will of his own, and the Bible describes his pervasive influence by calling him the god of this world.[2]

When God created the earth, he gave authority to mankind to govern the world. When mankind rebelled against God, we entered into Satan's domain, losing our authority to the devil. Now the world is a mess. Sickness and destruction are everywhere thanks to the will of Satan and the will of sinful man.

The kingdom of God is at hand, but where exactly is it? Jesus said the kingdom is found within people's hearts, and it

---

1 Matthew 6:9-10
2 2 Corinthians 4:4 ESV

comes to those who are violent—who take it by force.[3] We as the Church have played a lot of religious games, but we have spent little time or effort earnestly calling down God's kingdom to reign in our hearts.

I'm frightened by Christians who pray for "God's will," all while believing that the terrible things happening to them and the people they know are all a part of the will of God. Much of the Church has bought this lie. For this reason, we see little of God's will on earth, and an overwhelming amount of Satan's.

We can see this lie clearly illustrated when we use salvation as an example. The Church has pretty much embraced that salvation comes by repentance and belief in Jesus. But say you were preaching the gospel to me, trying to get me saved, and I responded:

"Why should I repent and ask Jesus to forgive me to be saved? If God wants to save me, why doesn't he just do it?"

"Because," you might say, "salvation is a free gift from God. He offers it to us, but we have to accept it. God allows us to choose him or not choose him. You don't get to experience salvation without surrendering to God and asking him to come into your heart. He won't force his way into a relationship with you; you have to invite him."

This is how salvation is explained by much of the Church. Why then, if we cannot experience salvation except by invitation—something God wants all men to experience[4]—does the Church believe that we will experience God's will in any area of our lives without a similar invitation? And what better way is there to start having experiences where God defines who he is to us than praying:

"God, I want you to show me who you are. I want you to replace the ideas I've thought about you with real experiences with you—experiences like those the earliest Church had in the

---

3 Luke 17:21-22 and Matthew 11:12
4 2 Peter 3:9

Bible. I don't want to know you as a picture I've imagined in my mind. I want you to define yourself to me."

From the night that God became my father, I began seeking him for who he is, actively suspending my assumptions about him. The next step in God defining himself to me was to learn to hear his voice. It started one evening at the house church.

—

I'm sitting on an ottoman in the middle of Grant and Rachel's living room. The couch is full. Worship ended only a few moments ago, and now we've gathered to pray. Grant speaks.

"I want everyone to ask the Holy Spirit what he wants us to pray for tonight. Just take a couple minutes to ask him, and then we'll share what we think he's saying."

This isn't the first time I've seen people asking the Holy Spirit questions or even saying something they felt like God told them. This is, however, the first time someone's asked me—in a direct, yet nonthreatening way—what God is saying. In the past, this would have made me nervous, activating my insecurities through my need to perform and prove myself holy. But God's love has transported me to a place of security. Everything feels new to me. Could hearing from God be simple? Is it possible to ask God a specific question and hear his response in a matter of minutes? I'm more than willing to try.

Across the living room, people are readying themselves to hear from God. Some bow their heads. Some close their eyes. Others keep their eyes open and simply stare at a point in the room. After glancing around for a posture to model, I decide to lower my head and close my eyes.

"Alright, Dad," I say in my mind. "What do you want us to pray for tonight?"

I concentrate. I clench my eyes with even more force. Two minutes of silence pass. I hear nothing.

"Okay, let's hear what everyone heard," says Grant.

One at a time, nearly every person in the room shares what they heard. Much of what the group says fits together, creating a theme for us to pray into.

After prayer finishes, I head into the bathroom. While washing my hands, I catch my reflection in the mirror. I study my eyes and think of the times I believe I heard clearly from God. There was the time I received salvation at church camp. Just a month ago, I heard God while Bob was giving me a hug. There are a handful of times I believe someone spoke to me a direct word from God. Thinking back, I feel grateful. I know so many Christians who've told me they've never clearly heard the voice of God. Yet, I can feel something pushing me toward this. My recent experiences with God have left me knowing there is more in him than I ever realized. I'm an explorer whose ship has crashed into a new continent. I'm enjoying the beach, but I know I can't stay here. There's more out there, much more I need to see.

The words of Jesus flitter in my mind.

Ask and it will be given. Seek and you will find. Knock and the door will be opened.

Whispering, I speak out-loud to God.

"Dad, I'm going to ask to hear your voice clearly. I'm going to keep asking, and I'm not going to get frustrated or give up; I'm just going to keep asking to be able to hear your voice clearly until I can. I know it's possible because Jesus could hear you clearly, and he's our example. The apostles of the early Church could hear you clearly. This crazy group of Christians can hear you clearly. I want to hear you clearly."

I dry my hands and leave the bathroom. After that night, each time I spend time with God, I ask to hear his voice clearly. Months go by.

I'm in Friday morning chapel at my college. It's November of my sophomore year. This semester, my church outgrew Grant and Rachel's living room and started meeting in a large classroom here at my university of all places. It takes me three minutes to walk to church on Sunday mornings. Caleb and I share a dorm with two other roommates. By now, I've had multiple conversations with Caleb, Jason, and Grant about hearing God's voice. Grant encouraged Caleb and I to take up two-way journaling as a way to practice hearing from the Holy Spirit.

"You start by writing down a question for God to answer," Grant said. "A good question to start with is, 'God, what do you think about me?' Then you wait and pay attention to any thoughts that pop in your head. Write down anything that comes to you, and keep writing if you get any more thoughts. A lot of times, God speaks to us in a quiet voice that sounds like our own thoughts, but if we write it down, then we can go back later and judge the things we thought God said with Scripture and with everything else God's said to us personally."

Caleb picked this practice up with gusto. I find him often at his desk, headphones on so no one disturbs him, writing lengthy conversations with the Holy Spirit in ink. It's been a dry process for me. I've faired better with what Grant encourages our church to do during praise and worship.

"Let the Holy Spirit lead you during our time of worship. During worship, you might get a small feeling or impression to do something, like to lift your hands or lay down on the ground or to sit down and pray or to read a passage in the Bible. It might be really simple, but if you feel like the Holy Spirit is pushing you to do something specific, I encourage you to follow him and take that small step. I've found that if I follow the first small leading of the Holy Spirit, he starts to give me more small steps and pretty soon he's leading me throughout the entire time of worship."

This connected with me. Praise and worship has always been my favorite part of church services, and I've often wondered how to go deeper with God during worship to experience more of him. For a few weeks now, I've tried my best to follow any impressions to worship God in specific ways during corporate worship. I don't hear God clearly in these moments, but I do feel like he's communicating to me. It's an unspoken language, and it reminds me of the one I've learned as a dancer.

In ballroom dancing, partners have specific roles. The "lead" is whoever is leading the dance; the "follow" is whoever is following the lead. In social dancing, nothing is choreographed. All movements are unplanned and unspoken. Partners don't discuss what move they want to do next as they're dancing. Instead, all necessary information is passed through a physical median—the points of contact at the hands, the follow's shoulder blade, and the lead's bicep. The lead's role is to plan out the dance and communicate the coming movements to the follow through subtle pushes and pulls. The follow's role is to concentrate on what's being communicated and to actively respond. If the follow is passive, expecting the lead to do all the work, the dance falls apart. If the follow matches the lead's energy, the two move as one unit. To do this with God is worship. He is the lead. I am the follow. I'm training to be sensitive to his movements, and my connection to him deepens as I follow him.

I ponder these things as the chaplain opens the service with prayer. On stage, our student worship band breaks into a praise song. I stand and sing and consider how the Holy Spirit might be leading me to worship. The first song and a half passes. I stand and sing and I raise my hands. The band transitions into the last song. Suddenly, I feel something. A small nudge. An inclination. Something inside me wants to kneel; a gentle push encourages me to plant my knees into the rough, navy blue chapel carpet.

I turn my head quickly to the left and right. I see exactly what I expected to see. Students and staff—most standing, several sitting, a few with raised hands. No one kneeling. If this was worship at my church, I wouldn't hesitate to kneel. Our services are flooded with a desire to worship God. My friends' expectation for God to show up is extreme; I'm swept up in that atmosphere. Chapel is different. Everyone shuffles in at 9:57, sings a few songs, hears a message, and shuffles out to their next class at 11:03. The experience is more polite than powerful. Sometimes I forget I'm even in a worship service for minutes at a time, my mind drifting through a stained-glass window into the open air. I'm not sure if I've ever felt the Holy Spirit leading me to do something during chapel, before this nudge that is—if this is even the Holy Spirit. I'm suddenly hyper-aware of my position on the front row. With rows of eyes staring at the back of my head, this doesn't feel like the place to make any sudden, unorthodox movements. And yet the nudge continues. I exhale a long and quiet, "Okay." Staring down a spot on the carpet, I try to look past my self-consciousness as I kneel to the ground.

The moment my knees land, a thought sparks in my brain.

I love you, the thought says.

Then more sparks.

I love spending time with you.

I'm at once entirely absorbed by the activity in my brain.

I love the way you worship.

Could these thoughts be from God? Is this him speaking to me? But they sound like my own thoughts. Concentrating, I hear my own speaking voice rambling off musings and calculations inside my mind. And these new thoughts share the same voice and the same headspace.

The new thoughts continue through worship and then through the message.

I've made you a forerunner.

As I try to sort my own thoughts from what God might be communicating to me, frustration builds in my mind. If this really is God speaking to me, how can I distinguish between my own thoughts and his?

Don't put me in a box.

What if God tries to tell me to do something, but then I don't do it cause I just thought it was a random thought I had? Is God going to judge me for not obeying him?

I'm going to ask you to do things that stretch you, that make you uncomfortable.

What if I believe one of these thoughts are from God, but it's really from me? Am I going to start doing weird stuff, believing it's something God wants me to do?

Chapel ends. Mentally preoccupied, I shuffle out of the service among a crowd of students. Standing on one side of the lobby, more thoughts ignite in my brain. The thoughts say things about students—different students in the lobby who are part of groups, talking and laughing or walking together toward the cafeteria. I'm hearing or thinking things about these people, about a dozen people, but I don't know why or where the thoughts are coming from. Maybe I'm just having strange thoughts. But what if they are from God? What would that mean—should I be running around the lobby right now telling everybody the God-thoughts I'm having about them? I don't know what to do, and now I'm frightened. What if these new thoughts don't stop? My brain feels like a train that jumped its rails, barreling uncontrollably to some sudden and terrible end. This is too much for me. Trying to stay calm, I make a straight line to the restroom.

I check the stalls, making sure the room is empty. I don't want anyone to see me as I question my own sanity. Wide-eyed, I stare at myself in the mirror.

"Okay God, I know I asked to hear your voice, but this is freaking me out," I whisper. "If this is you, make it stop."

I take a deep breath, and I close my eyes. I focus on what's happening in my mind. The new thoughts are gone. My brain has returned to normal. Relieved, I leave the restroom and head to the cafeteria.

It's less than a week later, and I'm feeling so guilty. I mean, seriously, what the heck is wrong with me? I ask God for months to speak to me, and the moment he does, I flip out and tell him to stop. Holy Spirit, I am sorry; would you please speak to me again?

—

Over time, God helped me become more confident in knowing his voice. I still have uncertainty at times whether something I'm hearing or feeling is from God or from me, but I've learned that God is extremely gracious towards me regarding this. If I need something confirmed to know it's from God, he confirms it in some way, often by speaking to me through someone else. I also am constantly checking anything I "hear" to make sure it is consistent with what God says in the Bible.

For most of my Christian life, I was frustrated by my inability to discern what God wanted me to do with my life or even my day. My definition of spiritual maturity was being able to hear specific instructions from God on what to do each moment of every day, and then following those instructions to the letter. But I wasn't able to hear God in that way, which added greatly to my feelings of spiritual inadequacy. So I settled for trying to hear his voice for just the big decisions of my life. Decisions like where I should go to college, what my career should be, and who I should marry. However, I couldn't hear God confidently for those either, which also added greatly to my feelings of spiritual inadequacy. In my mind, God had a mile long to-do list for me. I couldn't fully please God until I could hear what was on the list. Since I was too dumb to hear the things God wanted me to do, I was in constant doubt and fear that the things I was doing were wrong, no matter what they were. One day, I hoped, I would grow to become fully mature, able to hear from God clearly, and I would finally be able to live in a secure and confident way, knowing each step I take was planned out by God and then passed down to me.

However, after God became my dad, and after I did start to hear from the Holy Spirit, I was surprised at the kind of things he would say to me. It was more than surprising; it was paradigm shifting. His words changed everything I thought I knew about God and about my life.

When I first started to hear from God, almost everything he told me was about myself or about our relationship. I had thought he wanted me to hear his voice so I would be more effective at performing his will through specific tasks. But I found, more than anything else, he was interested in who I am. He spoke to me to change me, not to orchestrate my behavior.

One of the first times I experienced this was shortly after I told God in the restroom to stop speaking. My church had recently moved to its own building, and I was driving back to campus after a service. Right before pulling into the entrance of my university, I heard God speak in my mind.

I never wanted a robot. I never wanted a workhorse. I want a son.

I could have crashed my car due to my tears. My mindset shifted in a moment. I realized that there is no endless list of tasks with God. I was hiding from God behind my service for him, and he was trying to get me to slow down and be with him. That was the beginning of one of the hardest lessons I've learned in my spiritual walk: God is more interested in making me into the person he's called me to be than getting me to start doing specific acts. If my spirit, soul, and body become like God originally designed them, then I will naturally start to do the things he's called me to do. "Being" always comes before "doing."

I think this is why it took me so long to be able to hear

God's voice. For years, the only question I asked God was some version of "what should I do?" If he had answered me those questions, I could have kept hiding behind works; I might not have ever let him close enough to change my heart.

Once he started speaking change into my heart and mindset, he didn't let up. After leaving chapel one day, I was walking around the outside of the building toward my dorm when I heard him again.

You don't have to be successful.

One way I've learned to recognize the voice of the Holy Spirit is by the depth of meaning that the simple words can carry. For me, these words spoke to my fear of not measuring up to others. My whole life, it seemed, I carried the burden that I needed to look successful at all times. As my college days passed, this burden grew heavier as I felt like my life depended on whether or not I could leap straight into a prestigious, high-paying career the day after graduation. These words spoke to a deep fear of not being enough—a lie that I need to cover my personal inadequacy with ornaments of affluence. In that moment, I could feel for the first time that my ultimate fulfillment does not hinge on my ability to earn a position of prominence in the world. In that moment, I told myself that I could live in a shack in the woods and be happy. Even then, God's love and favor would be poured out on me, and he would still shape me into the person he made me to be. To this day, this is one of the most freeing thoughts I've ever held in my mind.

Around this same time, I became irritated with the mundane busyness of my life. As my love for praying and worshiping God grew, frustration with class, studying, and work grew. I saw the entirety of life falling into two categories. The first was the wondrous realm of God. The second was the tedious realm of chores. My destiny seemed to lie entirely in the first category. All else was a leech—stealing from the glory God intended to show me. Following this line of thought, I considered drastically shaping my life to cut away as much of the tedium as possible. I pictured myself with a long, gray beard living on some secluded mountain top or deep in a forest, only rising from prayer when my body demanded sustenance. I'd be my own version of Thoreau, only I'd be too busy praying to write a book about it. Far away from people and the endless distractions of society, I would be free to become my true self in God's presence alone.

I meditated on this one day in the woods close to campus, not far from where I used to yell at God. It was there that God spoke to me.

I did not create you to be a monk.

My mind reeled. Here I was, sketching out plans for spending the most time possible with God over the course of my life, and he snatched up my drawings and threw them in the garbage. I couldn't compute why God would discourage me from what I knew to be most important: being with him. He forced me to consider that perhaps there is some deeper meaning to be found in the second—what I considered lesser—category of life. A small shift occurred in how I viewed work and day-to-day tasks. Deep in my person, God planted a seed that would take years to grow into a fruitful tree—one that is still growing.

What I didn't realize during my monkish musings was that by isolating my spirituality from the realm of normal life, I was isolating God from that realm as well. I wanted to escape to heaven, not knowing that the earth is the Lord's and all that is in it.[5] God called me to be salt to the earth,[6] and I wanted to hide in the seasonings cabinet. By viewing God as active only in "spiritual" settings—church, retreats, mission trips—I placed him in a box that had nothing to do with my work, school, relationships, hobbies, family, community, or in essence, ninety percent of my life. I committed the great sin against my own heart: compartmentalization. I was therefore not a whole person but a

---

5 Psalm 24:1
6 Matthew 5:13

gross patchwork of the "holy" and "unholy." I was a fragmented person worshiping a fragmented God.

God's called me to be integrated. He's called me to surrender, to be fully his. To be fully God's is to be fully whole. Yet, I had a warped view of surrender for many years. Having grown up in church, I had a dominating image of what surrendering every part of my life to God should look like. This image was people, or positions, in the church—namely pastors, preachers, worship leaders, missionaries, Bible teachers—anyone whose occupation was "full-time ministry." I elevated these people because they were elevated by my community. As such, I assigned them a different class than other Christians. To me, these were the Christians that had truly surrendered every part of themselves and their lives to Christ. Consequently, deep in my person I held a twisted belief. If I ever surrendered all of myself to God, if I ever truly became "on fire for Jesus," then I would become a full-time minister—a full-time employee of a church or ministry. And since I did not hold one of these positions, and was not studying or training to occupy one, I unconsciously considered this proof that I was not, and would never be, completely surrendered to God and his will.

As I write this, I am literally thanking God that I did not try to become a pastor of a church. I remember about a dozen people telling me in high school that I should be a preacher because of my devotion to Jesus. I remember my internal struggle during my first semester at a Christian university, when I considered abandoning my business studies for a ministry degree so I could one day be the leader of a church. I wanted my life to matter; I wanted to be eternally significant. I didn't want to just be a churchgoer—a nice Christian who donates money to Jesus' real disciples who are actually making a difference in people's lives. I nearly bent to this religious pressure and jumped into church work. I would have if it wasn't for two things. First, in my pride and hunger for significance, I needed to be the boss of whatever I was involved in. Meaning, if I was going to go into full-time ministry, I needed to be the head-pastor of a church. I couldn't settle for being an employee of a ministry. Second—and inseparable from the first—deep down, I hated the thought of being the head-pastor of a church. It just looked like an annoyingly awful job to me. At the time, I judged this dislike as spiritual inadequacy on my part. However, I now know that being a head-pastor simply conflicted with who God made me to be.

I need to clarify a few points. I am not trying to degrade anyone who works full-time for a church or is studying to do so. I am saying that I viewed—and I believe many in the Church view—surrender to God as the act of throwing away the uniqueness of one's person and conforming to fit into an established and widely recognized, religious role. I've had many conversations with young Christians like me who are confused and frustrated. At one point in their life, they felt an incredible urge to serve God and others with their entire life; they experienced what they describe as "the call to ministry." And now, waist deep in the church world, they feel like they don't measure up, like they aren't cut out for the work, and they're guilt-ridden by the fact that their burning desire for ministry has all but dissipated.

The issue is simply that we as Christians take burdens on ourselves that God doesn't give us. We think surrender means becoming someone we are not, rather than letting God into every part of who we are. We think God's will is for us to hold an office, when it's actually for us to become his Bride. We think we can find significance in obtaining established positions recognized by the Church community, when significance only comes through intimacy with God.

As such, we have to remember that God's desire for us is to know him. The work he requires of us is "to believe in the one he has sent."[7] In the book of Galatians, Paul writes at length

---

7 John 6:29 NIV

about the trap of believing that we can be justified or become pleasing to God by our works.

"Did you receive the Spirit by works of the law or by hearing with faith? Are you so foolish? Having begun by the Spirit, are you now being perfected by the flesh?"[8]

The answer to that last question is an unequivocal no. We receive salvation and the Holy Spirit by faith; we are perfected by faith as well. Any attempt to make ourselves pleasing to God by our works rather than our faith is an act of our flesh and is outside of the will of God. That includes shoving ourselves into a religious mold or trying to become someone we think is holier than us. But when we believe in the one whom he sent, we are transformed in his presence into who we are meant to be.

When I believed God's will was for me to do specific actions—which I had to decipher in order to accomplish—I was a paralyzed person, afraid to take any path because I couldn't be sure if it was the one and only "right one." God's true will—his desire for us to be close to him and to become who he originally designed us to be—is not paralyzing. It's liberating. If I'm seeking to be close to God, then I'm in his will and there is nothing to worry about. If God is turning me into who he wants me to be, then my life is a process and not a box to be checked off. Whether I turn left or right, I can trust that God will use my circumstances to make me more like him. And as I become more like him, the types of things God loves to do will pour out of me naturally.

This is why the Holy Spirit's words were so surprising to me. This is the paradigm shift I referred to earlier. I assumed all God wanted to tell me was what I should do and what I am currently doing wrong. Instead, he wanted to tell me who I am to him and who he wants to be to me. God invited me into intimacy before action. Not long after beginning to hear from

---

8 Galatians 3:2-3 ESV

the Holy Spirit, I realized how foreign and uncomfortable this intimacy was for me.

One day while praying, a scene—like a scene from a movie—started to play in my imagination. A large table covered in food sat in the dining room of a warm, cosy house. The Father sat at the head of the table, and he invited me to come sit next to him to eat and talk. I did so, but I felt my self-consciousness growing each second I sat at that table. It was like I was eating and conversing with the queen of England—I feared appearing uncouth, undignified. As such, I was guarded, overthinking my every movement and word. Not long after sitting, I decided it was time to leave. I hadn't yet made a fool of myself in front of God, and I wanted to make my escape before I did. Plus, my back was feeling stiff; I wanted to find somewhere to relax and be myself for a while after such a mentally taxing meal. I politely said my goodbyes and pushed back my chair. As I walked away from the table, however, I heard the Father calling to me, inviting me to sit next to him and dine with him again. I looked back but stood frozen. The Father smiled and gently motioned with his hand for me to come back to the table. I didn't want to be rude, but I also didn't want to sit back down again.

"It's nice of him to invite me, but I can't sit at the table all day," I thought to myself. "I already sat there for a while today. Now I need to go relax and do other stuff. There's no way I could sit there being polite and proper forever." The scene ended.

I believe the Holy Spirit was using my imagination to speak to me, and the message was clear. God was inviting me to sit at his table, right next to him, forever. And I was only comfortable with limited periods of closeness. I only wanted to be with him for a time. I would get up from his table, then go back to his table, then get up from his table. To remain seated next to him all day, every day, felt grossly impossible. At the time, I couldn't conceive of the intimacy that he desired. I didn't know how to be comfortable with God for lengthy periods of time—I didn't even know that was possible. In the next chapter, I will explain why this felt impossible and what changed. But for now, I will simply argue this point: consistent intimacy with God is possible for every believer.

Christians too often view the first disciples of Jesus as having a sort of spiritual leg-up to us because they got to walk with Jesus when he was physically on earth as a man. But that's exactly the opposite of what Jesus said. He told his disciples that it was better for them that he goes away so he can send them the Holy Spirit.[9] Either the Holy Spirit is better for us than Jesus in physical form or Jesus was a liar. Much of the Church acts like Jesus was lying; they don't believe that they have more access to God than the disciples did while they were physically walking with Jesus.

Potentially, each of today's believers can have more access to God and the kingdom of heaven than those who walked with Jesus at the time of his earthly ministry. That is because as a man, Jesus was limited in his ability to connect with, pay attention to, and disciple each of his followers. Think of a single babysitter taking care of twelve kids at the same time (and Jesus had many more followers than just the Twelve.) Little one-on-one time can occur with that ratio. I am not undercutting the importance of Jesus' physical time on earth or the mentoring of his disciples in any way. But I am agreeing with Jesus when he said, "It is better that I go…" Here's why I believe it is better:

The Holy Spirit's presence and love is infinite. As the Church, we have generally grasped the concept of the infinite love of God, at least to a degree. However, we are lacking greatly in our experiential knowledge of the presence of the Holy Spirit. Sometimes Christians say things like, "God is everywhere," but to most people, that sentiment is no more useful than to say,

---

9 John 16:7

"God is nowhere." That's because we don't experience God as if he truly was everywhere—with us at all times. As the Church, more of us than not view God as a parent who lives on the other side of the planet. Sometimes he sends gifts, occasionally he may write a letter or even call us on the phone, but he isn't close enough to embrace us. We may believe otherwise theologically. We may talk about the constant presence of God. But without experiencing the presence of the Holy Spirit, our hearts will never be able to view God as more than an absent parent.

The Holy Spirit is God, and he comes to live inside of us by invitation. Walking with the Spirit is greater than walking with Jesus as a man. The Holy Spirit gives one-on-one attention to all of us. He is always close enough to personally guide us, teach us, renew us, and embrace us. The disciples of Jesus found this out when Jesus fulfilled his word and sent them the Holy Spirit after leaving earth. They experienced the infinite love and infinite presence of the Holy Spirit. That's why so many of them were able to bear brutal persecution—something they could not bear when they physically walked with Jesus. Truly, nothing could separate them from the constant love of God.

My pastor, Grant, illustrates it in this way. Imagine an old, medieval kingdom with both knights and princes who serve a noble king. The knights and the princes have similar roles and perform many of the same duties. They both train together for battle, they both are welcome at court, and they both receive orders from the king to fulfill. With all their similarities though, the difference between a knight and a prince is immense. The knight serves the king out of respect and loyalty. The prince serves his father out of love; he has a close relationship with the king. When the day's work ends, the knight returns to his own home. Yet, the prince remains in his father's house at all times. The prince has familiarity and access to the king that far surpasses that of the knight.

Many Christians resign themselves to knighthood even

though their true identity is that of a prince. For years, my relation to God was almost entirely of service and duty. Even worse, I felt like the King consistently judged my best service as inadequate. So I exhausted myself in a never-ending cycle of burdensome effort and an overwhelming sense of failure. As the Father's love undermined the lies I believed for so long, I gaped in awe at the meaning of the words in Romans 8:1. "There is therefore now no condemnation for those who are in Christ Jesus." I felt the Spirit pulling me toward the deep mysteries of Galatians 4:6-7. "And because you are sons, God has sent the Spirit of his Son into our hearts, crying, 'Abba! Father!' So you are no longer a slave, but a son, and if a son, then an heir through God." Hesitantly, I responded to his leading.

Not long after seeing God invite me to his table, another movie played out in my imagination during a time of prayer. I was in a tower of a large castle. The room around me was full of shelves and tables covered in maps and books and scrolls. Not far from me, three men stood around a table with a large map sprawled out between them. They were in animated discussion. They spoke loudly, pointing to places on the map and motioning toward the open window close by. It became clear to me that they were the lords of the land illustrated on the map; they were discussing their plans for governing it. I felt the significance of the room and the decisions that were made there on a regular basis. Suddenly, the three men turned to me and fervently motioned for me to join them. The words of Jesus came to my mind: "No longer do I call you servants, for the servant does not know what his master is doing; but I have called you friends, for all that I have heard from my Father I have made known to you."[10] I walked to the table, and the men immediately ushered me into their discussion, explaining to me their plans and ideas and asking for my input.

---

10 John 15:15 ESV

During my college years, my heart gradually accepted more and more of the truth of my position in God's kingdom thanks to the sacrifice of Jesus Christ. I grew in greater confidence in hearing from the Holy Spirit and also in walking closely with God throughout the day. Never had I consistently experienced more joy and less fear. Surrounded by a supportive church family and encouraging friends, my mind surged with incredible dreams and adventures for my life. I knew I was destined to accomplish great things for the kingdom of God. I was confident that God had an exciting plan for me, and as graduation neared, I eagerly waited for him to unveil the steps to my glorious, ordained path. My hands were open, and I could already feel the weight of the unimaginable purpose about to be handed to me. Then something happened. Something I did not anticipate. Something that completely rewrote my ideas on destiny and God's will.

—

"Come in. It's good to see you again."

I follow Adam into his office and take in the room with quick turns of my head. Each corner displays modern style and impeccable tidiness. The desk is clear of clutter. A row of books on government, finance, leadership, and strategies for humanitarian efforts protrude from the far back wall. An attractive house plant grows under open blinds.

"That's a cool looking plant."

"Thanks. My kids planted it for me."

Looking at Adam, I'm struck by how perfectly his office fits him. It's more a mirror than a room, reflecting his own precision and deftness. Just under thirty, Adam is a respected, successful young professional sporting a clean hair cut, a wrinkle free button-up shirt, and one of those sleek watches with rectangle hands and little unmarked dots where numbers are supposed to go. Before him stands an underemployed, recent college-grad with hair that speaks of a difficulty in remembering to visit the barber, a shirt that is tucked in for the sole-purpose of concealing a lack of ironing, and a digital watch speckled with dots of white paint. Our juxtaposition reinforces my understanding of who Adam is. Adam is a man capable of handling every aspect of life that I can't. He can wake up early enough to exercise while it's still dark outside. He can shave without cutting himself. He can court a woman to marriage. But most importantly, he can follow a clear path that leads him to a prominent position and a successful career. That's why I'm here.

Seven months ago, I graduated college with high hopes for my future. My hopes were partially built upon natural optimism but mostly upon a couple things that happened before I graduated.

First, with less than a year left until graduation, I started to pray about what to do after college. I was seeking a career in the public sector, leaning toward city management, and I was thinking about getting a master's degree. I didn't know where I should go to accomplish this. So, I asked God where he wanted me to go. I thought there was somewhere in the country he wanted me to work and to study, somewhere he could plant me to grow into my destiny.

I prayed about my future while driving one day, and I felt the Holy Spirit speak to my heart.

Where do you want to go?

"Where do *I* want to go?" I thought. I hadn't given my preference any consideration. I was waiting for God to tell me where he wants me to go. The concept of God asking for my input was still strange to me. I wasn't sure; I hadn't thought about where I wanted to go. I'd only been thinking in terms of where and what would be best—best for expanding the kingdom of God and for propelling me into success.

I assigned the minimum mental focus needed to steer my car; the rest I turned toward examining my own heart and mind. What first came to my attention were the answers so many people that I knew had given to that question. California, Paris, England, New York City, Colorado, Singapore—there were numerous exciting places I heard again and again in conjunction with "I want to live in..." Like a flock of birds, locations fluttered across my mental view. But where was my answer?

I tried imagining myself living somewhere—anywhere—shooting out roots, becoming part of a land, grafting myself to a community. Splotchy and out of focus, the image told me that I had little experience with claiming a location as my own. I moved but once my whole life, from Texas to Oklahoma, but I wasn't sure if I had ever lived in either. I was always so focused on the future, so concerned with where to go next; I hardly paid attention to wherever I happened to be. I felt like a perpetually transient being: a ghost, haunting cities and schools and places of work.

I thought of statistics I heard about people moving more often now than ever before. I thought of how almost everyone I met could talk incessantly about places they wanted to move to or visit. The ultimate dream for many my age was to be able to continuously travel, to always be skipping about the earth on a never ending tour of the world.

"Nearly everyone," I thought, "regardless of where they live, wishes they could be somewhere else."

Suddenly, I wished I could just be. I wanted the ghost to take human form, solidify, and for once in his life, to belong somewhere. Then it came to me. I knew where I wanted that to happen.

"Can I stay here?" I asked God. "I like this place. I have friends here. I have a church family that I actually feel connected to, and I've never had that before. I feel you are doing something in this city. I don't know what it is, but just driving around

I get the sense that something big is getting ready to happen here. I think you are setting things up for a great move of your Spirit. I'm starting to feel like I really do live here, as if I'm a part of this place, and I want to experience what that's like."

As the words floated from my mouth, a tide of peace rose in my stomach. I felt like the Father was patting me on the back with one hand and giving me a thumbs-up with the other. I knew then that God would give me a way to live here. I knew then that he would take care of me in this place. I knew then that somewhere in the city my destiny lay buried, and God was going to help me uncover it. I didn't know what my life would look like after graduation, but I knew where I would be living.

The second event to take place occurred less than two months before graduation. I had no job lined up after college and no place to live. At the beginning of the fall—the beginning of my last semester—I spent hours applying to full-time positions at different local governments. I never received a response. Now it was nearly mid-November. My last semester closed at the end of December. With final projects looming, I didn't have enough time for another round of applications.

Worse, my housing situation added to the intensity and subtracted from my time. For my last year and half of college, I lived in a rented house with three other guys. One of them got married and moved out at the beginning of the semester. At the end of October, another guy decided he was moving out. My last roommate and I quickly calculated that we couldn't afford to split a house that originally had four lodgers. We decided to move out at the end of November. I prepared for my impending move, three weeks away, with no idea where to move to. Without a full-time job, I couldn't afford my own apartment, and I still had over a month before finishing college.

I figured I could finish the semester by sleeping on friend's couches. But what would I do when I graduated? With no job or a place to live, I'd have to move back to Texas and live with my parents. I knew I was incredibly blessed to even have that as an option. But, I also knew where I wanted to live. I felt like God had made me a promise—to help me live and grow in Oklahoma City. I felt God affirmed my decision to stay here; I could still feel him affirming that decision, even though I had no means to make it happen.

The next Monday, with these burdens heavy on my mind, I walked into a small classroom where a few friends and I met once a week to pray. As usual, our prayer group spread out across the room to find a spot to pray individually before we began praying together. Sitting on the floor, my back to the wall, I spoke to God in a whisper.

"Dad, if this is a good thing for me, if you want me to be able to stay here, you're going to have to make it happen. I'm out of time and I don't know what to do. I need a job and I need a place to live. I know you know what's best for me, and I know you're always taking care of me. Whatever happens, I'm going to trust you."

A few minutes later, my friends and I sat in a circle and prayed together. When asked for a prayer request, I quickly explained how I needed a place to live. They prayed for me, asking God to give me a great place to live and the provision to afford it. Our meeting ended. I picked up my backpack and left the room.

Walking down the hall, I pulled out my phone to take it off silent, and saw I had missed a call. It was from Jason. He had called me a few minutes ago, the same time I was being prayed for. It seemed like forever since I last talked to Jason. He attended a different church now, so I didn't see him nearly as much anymore. I attended his wedding the past summer. I knew he and his wife had an apartment in the city, and I knew he was busy starting a new career. I stepped outside to call him back.

"Hey Jason," I said.

"Hey Reese! How are you doing?" he replied.

"Yeah, good. I'm doing okay; how are you?" I asked.

"I'm doing great," he said. "Listen, I have a question I need to ask you. Emily and I are buying a house. It's a two-story house, there are three extra rooms upstairs, and we want to rent out at least two of them. We want to rent them out to friends, so do you think you'd be interested in taking one of the rooms? We're moving into the house in just a couple of weeks. You don't have to move in that early, but it's available if you want it."

He then followed this up by telling me how much the room would cost. It was a third of what I'd be paying for my own apartment. His question stunned me. In a few moments, I gathered my senses and gave Jason an emphatic yes. Then I explained to him my situation—he knew none of it—and told him how God answered a prayer while it was still being prayed.

After this, the road rolled out before me like bricks falling from heaven. Jason and Grant were both friends with a few guys starting a business together—a virtual reality arcade. I received a job offer without having to interview; I started the day after my last final. It was only part-time, but it was fun and paid better than any part-time job I'd heard of. My university kept me on as a tutor and gave me a raise once I graduated. By mid-January, I landed another part-time job as an administrative assistant in an office two minutes from my new house.

I was doing it. I was living in Oklahoma City, self-sufficient for the first time in my life. God opened all the doors. All I had to do was say yes and walk through them. I was more than optimistic—I was thrilled. I felt like I had caught all of God's blessing and there wouldn't be enough to go around for others. Cheap living with great roommates. Check. Plenty of friends. Check. A fantastic church community. Check. Plenty of money. Half-check.

Although I was genuinely happy to be paying my bills, I would have preferred to be able to save money as well, especially since I planned to return to school for my master's degree. But that was a small matter. I knew I wouldn't be working part-time jobs forever. God gave me a door to live in OKC—beyond a doubt he would keep opening doors to my destiny.

Thus was January. My mood hit an all-time high around the first of February. Then began the steady decline.

I had a lot of free time. Even with three jobs, I wasn't quite working full-time; some weeks I worked as little as twenty-five hours. So, I found myself with numerous empty hours to fill. At first, I enjoyed the time immensely. I prayed, I read, I hung out with friends, I exercised. I did whatever I felt like doing, whatever was natural. But slowly, my relationship with my time shifted toward anxiety. When I was a student, there was always a goal my life arched toward. Free time—whole summers worth of free time—never bothered me because it was a scheduled break along my path to graduating, to completing my goal. That was no longer the case. I still had a goal; I just wasn't moving toward it. Without saving money for grad school, without possessing a job that could help launch me directly into my desired career, I felt like I was running in place. I worked; time passed; I never took a single step toward the end of the road.

So, I decided to use my free time to jumpstart my future. I read. I made connections. I practiced various skills. But in this, the anxiety grew exponentially worse. A seed of doubt, laying dormant till this point, took root. The doubt came in the form of a question: what if being a city manager isn't what I was made to do? I wanted badly to hold on to my goal. I feared the listlessness that could set in if I lost it. But I couldn't stop the doubt. Uncertainty pushed through my mind's soil, growing into a full bloom.

Unsure whether it was my true destiny, I could no longer charge unshakably toward a career in the public sector. I changed tactics. I decided to use my free time to explore different interests and careers. I thought dipping my toes in a multitude of waters would better help me claim my pool. I continued to look into the public sector, but I added entrepreneur, author, musician, dance instructor, massage therapist, videographer, teacher, nonprofit manager, nutritionist, chef, lottery winner, and a host of others to my list of careers to explore.

I thought this would reduce my fear of choosing the wrong path for my life. I figured after a little bit of research and testing, I could start crossing out whole fields and narrow my focus down to the one purpose God made me for. The opposite occurred. As I unfurled the scroll of life's possibilities, it fell from my hand, rolling out an infinite trail behind it. This was not a liberating or exciting discovery. It absolutely petrified me. I desperately needed to find my destiny—the one true path God intended for me—and now the ten roads I was trying to choose from multiplied into thousands. As my interests and possible careers grew steadily in number, so my uncertainty and unease grew in quantity. I stood at an intersection of infinite trail heads, paralyzed by indecision. I couldn't explore my options freely. Any step toward a path, however casual and noncommittal, filled me with overwhelming doubt. A step in the wrong direction was a step away from my true destiny. Whether writing, practicing piano, reading about local government, or calculating the cost of massage therapy school, every action was haunted by a recurring question. What if this isn't the best thing I could be doing with my time?

As such, I lost my ability to focus. Caught between too many decisions, fearful of making the wrong one, I stopped making decisions. I slept in. I watched TV. I sat on my bedroom floor and stared off into space, lost in a tangled mess of conflicting thoughts. I couldn't understand what God was doing. I thought he was going to lead me into an important and exciting life. I thought he had one ordained goal for me, my life purpose, that he was supposed to reveal to me or at least direct me toward one step at a time. I had run out of steps. There were no more in sight. I was glued to a stationary bike. For a time, I tried changing my situation by applying to more full-time, better paying jobs, so I could at least start saving up money for whatever it was I would one day decide to do with my life. But my attempts were fruitless, and I soon gave up trying. What I feared, I became. Listlessness.

I wanted to give up on the idea of destiny, long-term goals, ambition—become an unconcerned drifter, happy to receive whatever life happened to give, void of the desire for advancement. But even in my discouraged state, an invisible force continued to pull my psyche toward visions of grandeur. The force that left me restless in my listlessness was none other than comparison.

As I spun my wheels without destination, many of my friends were accepting well-paying positions within their chosen field, getting engaged, and buying houses—all in a short period of time. Within the same short period of time, I sat on my bedroom floor, broke and single, staring listlessly at the ceiling—a harsh juxtaposition to say the least.

Pride spoke to me at this time. It told me I deserved more—that I was smarter, superior to my friends in every way. It told me that life had made a mistake, dealing the worthiest amongst us a pitiable hand. Yet, insecurity spoke to me in the same moment.

"If you're so smart and capable," it said to me, "How come you can't land a full-time job or even choose a career path?"

This force of comparison, a double-stranded rope of pride and insecurity, dragged me alternately between frenzies of maniac effort and doldrums of forlorn acceptance. It was one of my states of frenzy that brought me to Adam's office.

I became connected to Adam through Jason. He told me about Adam, and I began to wish that I was Adam. CEO of a nonprofit and governor appointee to a state board—Adam was a shining light bulb of success, drawing me like a moth. I jumped at my first chance to meet him, accompanying Jason to help move Adam's parents into their new home. I thought he could be useful to me. Through Adam, I hoped to gain access to a world of significance, a place where my efforts were channeled towards one important and clearly defined goal. The meeting I scheduled at his office was to me a golden door. I desperately hoped to find my path on the other side.

As we settle into a pair of seats next to a window, Adam asks me about my work. Struggling to conceal my desperate intent for this meeting—refraining from shouting, "PLEASE GIVE ME A JOB! I'M IMPORTANT! I WANT MY LIFE TO MATTER!"—I open up to Adam about how I'm trying to find my path in life. I tell him how I expected God to lay out a clear direction for my life and career yet it hasn't happened. I tell him how I want to find the first steps toward a worthy goal, something I can put my entire being into over the course of my life—a work that matters and provides for me the deep satisfaction of making a difference in the world. I wait for Adam's reply. I'm anticipating a "You can find that here! Can you start in two weeks?" or at least a "You should talk to my friend that owns/ runs an important organization! They need smart, ambitious guys like you—I'll put in a good word for you!"

"How old are you, Reese?" Adam's words are slow and deliberate; his eyes look soft to me, tinged with kindness and sincerity.

"I'm twenty-two."

"When I was twenty-two, I had just quit my job in the Air Force. I was waiting tables, trying to provide for my family and going to college at the same time. I had a great career lined up for me in the Air Force, but I felt like God told me my time there was done. It was like he took away all the interest I had in that career. He told me to quit and go to school. I had no idea why. I didn't know what I was going to do with my degree when I finally finished school."

I'm bewildered. I assumed a man like Adam had a clear

career path in mind from the age of eighteen. Seeing him in his office, I thought he had been taking calculated steps toward this specific position since he was an adult.

"Everywhere I have been, and where I am now, is only owed to me trusting God to take care of me and being faithful with whatever he gives me to do at the time. I learned to be content in Jesus, no matter what my work was."

Content. That's a word I hear Christians throw around a lot. Now it sticks out to me only because I'm dreadfully aware of it's polar opposite: discontent. It's apparent to me now that discontentment with my work has grown into discontentment with my life. What I want is a work that makes me content, and therefore, a life I'm content with.

"Think about it this way," he continues. "If the purpose of life is to know God, and to make him known to others, then that means that how your character is being built is more important than the work that you do. God wants to develop our heart and our character so that we can know him more. When we know God better, we are better at helping others know God. If your focus is the importance of what you are doing, the impact your work is having, then you will always become discontent.

"Take my job for example. I lead an organization that helps move people out of homelessness. Some people might think I have guaranteed job satisfaction because my job is to help people. But by the world's definition of success, I won't complete my end goal until I eliminate homelessness and the threat of homelessness. That will never happen. Poverty has been an issue for all of human history, and it isn't something I could lead an organization to completely solve. If I believe the purpose of my work is to accomplish an important end goal, then I will never be satisfied because there will always be more I haven't done. But if I ask God to use my work to develop my heart and my character, then I can be successful every day. Because no matter whether I'm succeeding or failing in the world's eyes, I'll be accomplishing the true purpose of life by becoming more like God in order to know him more."

My heart burns with an undefined, inner conflict. Adam's words feel true to me—to an extent—but something inside of me wars against them. Is he telling me that my search for a grand destiny is no more than a self-satisfying delusion? That, I don't know if I can accept. I can't leave here resigned to the current state of my life.

"Then what do you think I should do?" I ask Adam. "I'm working three part-time jobs, and I don't like any of them anymore. They feel beneath me. I have a college degree, and I'm wiping down tables and cleaning the bathroom of an arcade. I've tried applying to full-time jobs, and it hasn't come of anything."

Adam answers my question by reiterating what he's already said. His words carry the deep conviction of a man who's followed his own advice and still believes it's the answer that young, ambitious men like me need.

"Every day you go into work, ask God how he wants to use that day to develop your heart and your character. Steward what God's given you to do. If you are faithful with what he's given you, he will move you to bigger things. And stop thinking that your work is supposed to give you contentment. Be content in Jesus, and you will be content no matter what you are doing."

Unsure if it will work, I tell Adam I will follow his advice. Later in the day, I'm praying in my room about these things. My mind is still troubled by the idea of destiny. I wanted Adam to help me find my destiny, something I could spend my entire life working towards, something to successfully accomplish moments before passing from this life, something that would consistently give me a sense of importance for all of my days on earth. Thinking about how differently our meeting went than I expected, I realize that what I wanted from Adam perfectly parallels what I want from God.

I want God to bless me with a prestigious, straight-forward

career path that makes me feel significant. I thought God wanted to give me that. The fact that he hasn't is what led me to the frustrated, dissatisfied state that I'm in today. As this crux comes into focus, I hear the voice of the Holy Spirit, his thoughts, ignite in my brain.

If you never get to do anything important looking—if you work low-level, part-time jobs for the rest of your life—will I be enough for you? If you remain single for the rest of your life, will I be enough for you? Am I all you need to be satisfied?

As these questions come to the front of mind, I'm struck with an inconsistency in my own faith. At the beginning of this year, if someone were to ask me if God was all I needed, I would have answered with an exuberant "Yes!" In my mind, I've always believed that God was all a person needed. Now, I realize my heart has a different answer.

"I don't know," it says. "I don't know if I could be okay with that. I don't know if I could work a boring job my whole life and still be satisfied. I don't know if I could be single my whole life and still be satisfied. I'm really not sure if you, by yourself, are enough for me."

But I want him to be enough for me. I want to be content no matter what my circumstances are and no matter what my work looks like. I want to be content in Jesus. So, I make the decision to follow Adam's advice. I decide to start asking God to use my current jobs to develop my heart and character, to bring me into a closer relationship with him.

By the end of the week, my life is already starting to feel entirely different. I'm enjoying my work again. I no longer feel crushing insecurity when I think about what my friends are doing. I can recognize how God is using my situation to make me a humbler, less self-absorbed person. This character arch shades every menial task with deeper meaning. And the best change by far: a sapling of contentment takes root in my heart. Soon, I hope, I'll be able to unreservedly say that God is enough for me. That he alone, without anything or anyone else, is enough for me.

———

What Adam handed me that day was nothing like what I was looking for. He gave me advice, but what I wanted was a clear path to success—a golden door to affluent opportunities. But what he gave me was better. For I did not understand the reason I wanted that path. I did not know an aching thirst for satisfaction was driving me to find it. The insatiable hunger of an empty heart—I have seen now what that does to a person. A man tries to fill the void with relationships, with notoriety, with accomplishments, with wealth. Yet each success is devoured by his cavernous soul, like pennies dropped into a bottomless well. In the autumn of his life, he sits upon a hill of bounties his work has stacked up for him. Agitated with longing, he peers from its great height only to realize with despair, there is nothing left on the landscape to be gathered.

We find satisfaction in God alone, or we find nothing. We find significance in God alone, or we find nothing. When we are called to be crucified with Christ, that also means the death of our concept of success. It was a painful process, but if God did not kill my pride and selfish ambition, I would still be living in a delusion today.

The delusion I lived in, and I believe many in the Church live in, is this: God wants us to become important for him. We often take messages of the world—"Live your dream!", "Climb the ladder!", "Become someone that others wish they were!"— and slap a Jesus fish sticker on them—"Live your dream, for Jesus!", "Climb the ladder, for Jesus!", "Become someone that others wish they were, for Jesus!"

I truly believed it was my destiny to become successful and important in the eyes of others. I thought God wanted me to do that, because then I would best be able to serve him and usher in his kingdom from such a successful and important position. By focusing on my success, I was missing my true destiny, a destiny that can be fully encapsulated in one word: intimacy. There is no higher calling than to know God, to be with him face to face. I know now that the only thing my life needs in order to have significance is worship. If I have drawn close to God, beheld him, worshiped him, then I've accomplished what is most important. If we can grasp the identity God imparts to us as his intimate friend, then we will never be insecure in our significance.

I do believe God moves us to do specific work. I believe that there are dreams in people's hearts that were placed there by God. But these dreams are only to be pursued out of a place of intimacy with God. When I focus more on the dream than on God, my heart begins to worship the dream over God. As such, my identity becomes the dream and my own ability to accomplish it. When my worship is directed purely toward Jesus, then Christ becomes my identity. We must never forget that God longs to be with us, and out of a place of intimacy, he longs to partner with us—working and accomplishing with us and through us.

He never says, "Go do this, and when you finish, come back and I'll give you something else to do." Any dream or vision for our lives given to us by God is an invitation to do something with him—to get to spend time with him and know him better—not a command to be carried out apart from him.

And so, because of the wonderful love of God, my destiny rose higher. Not to do, but to become. Not to accomplish, but to worship. My sense of significance increased because intimacy with God deepened. My soul feels as large and as grand as the whole earth itself, forever blessed to encircle the Sun whose gaze leaves me teeming with life.

But this intimacy is only possible with trust. For many

years, I worshiped God and served him while trusting him very little. I had next to no power to develop trust in God—I was even unaware that I lacked trust. But he was too loving to leave me hurt and defensive. He was too good not to point out the roots of my mistrust and too caring not to tear them out.

Chapter 4

In which I cry while I'm writing.

One time, in college, I had a crush on a girl. It began during my first visit to a new coffee shop close to campus. Pushing my way through the door, stepping into a haze of nutty tones and spicy scents, the barista greeted me with:

"You look familiar! Is your name Reese? I think I have friends that know you."

And that was all it took. In a few moments, the coffee shop became the most interesting place I had ever visited. For many weeks, you could find me perched behind a corner table, laptop and textbooks sprawled before me. There I sat, burning my tongue on fresh steeped tea, ignoring my homework to stare wistfully through the glass pane of the shop's front door, hoping to catch her in view, walking across the parking lot to begin a shift. But she wasn't working that day. She didn't work much it seemed, or by bad luck I caught the shop at all the wrong times. Because, although I waited for hours almost daily—eternally nursing a single cup of coffee or tea—I hardly saw her there.

But the days I did see her. Those days—well, those days weren't all that different. The last thing I wanted to do was appear creepy (an area in which I already felt like I was failing, considering the fact that I was sitting in a coffee shop for hours hoping she would appear). As such, I barely talked to her or even looked her way when she was there. Eventually though, our short moments spent in conversation added up, minute by minute, until its quantity endowed me with the courage I needed.

In order to ask her for her number, I wanted the shop to be empty. Unbeknownst to him, I stared intently at the single other customer, seated close to the bar, trying to will him to finish his coffee and abandon his post. I just needed him to leave before anyone else walked in. My heart beat faster with each passing second, in fear that my window of opportunity was closing. Then suddenly, after ages upon eons, he stood up, dropped his paper cup into a recycling bin, and swung open the front door. When it shut behind him, the coffee shop was nearly empty. Only me, and the girl behind the bar.

"Hey, um, I was wondering if I could possibly, uh, get your phone number, so I could, you know, call or text you, so um, that way we could, um, you know, hang out sometime."

"Oh! Um. Sure."

After she answered my stuttering, nearly frantic request, I drove away high on my own hopes. For I had her number, and soon, her heart. Except, it didn't turn out that way. We never hung out—never went on a date. She was always busy when I asked. Evidently, she was much busier than I was, too busy to nervously wait around hoping that I would show.

I didn't give up. I had one move left to make. I knew the coffee shop owner from my hours clocked in the shop. One day, I asked her if I could host a social dance at her establishment. She thought it was a great idea. So did I. All my college friends were invited, including those particular mutual friends. Late on a Friday night, one of my older sisters—recently moved to OKC—and I walked into the coffee shop, ready to teach a beginner's East Coast Swing lesson to anyone there. And she was there.

I got to dance with her, so technically my plan succeeded. After the dance, however, my sister spelled out a hard truth that I was not yet able to read myself.

"I saw you dancing with the girl you told me about," she said. "She isn't interested in you."

"Oh," I said.

And thus a harmless crush passed without me appearing too creepy—hopefully—and without too much disappointment.

There are moments in our lives when something we see or experience becomes imprinted on our minds. Our memory paints the ceilings of our brains like the Sistine Chapel, with great murals of dramatic scenes looming above our thoughts. Months after my visits to the coffee shop, and after any feelings associated with the location had faded, an image remained in my mind.

Me—waiting at a table—hour after hour—hoping—always hoping—that someone would arrive.

Over time, the image morphed, as our memories often do, and more recent experiences shaped the pictures of the past. I can still see that image, but I am no longer the one sitting at the table.

Instead, I see Jesus—waiting at a table—hour after hour—day after day—hoping—longing—for me to arrive.

This is one of the many ways I see God's pursuit of me. He is more patient than I am busy. And he doesn't love me for a season but for eternity, with life-sacrificing abundance.

As Christians, we hear about the love of God often. I found, though, that there is a difference between knowing someone loves you and knowing you can trust their character. As much as I was told to trust God, as much as I wanted to trust him, my heart was riddled with wounds from my past—wounds that told me there is safety in distance.

I have written how wrong thoughts, wrong beliefs about God and ourselves, keep us on the outskirts of the kingdom of heaven—lost—unable to find the way to our true King and the truest expression of the life he calls us to live. But we as humans are more than our thoughts, more than our deepest held beliefs. We are emotional beings, as well as intellectual beings. Our hearts are as vulnerable to poisonous feelings as our minds are to poisonous lies. They can hardly be separated, as our feelings affect thoughts and our thoughts affect feelings. But too often the Church forgets or denies this reality, choosing to focus entirely on the health of one's intellect and not on the health of one's emotions.

For I can teach doctrine, but how do I teach someone's heart to stop hurting? I can stimulate the mind, but how do I enliven a soul that is hardened, unfeeling, or dead. As many things do, it seems all but impossible. Our wrong feelings about God, like our wrong thoughts, keep us from God. And if we are far from God, how can change occur?

But even this conundrum is overcome by the love of Jesus Christ. And if he bridged the widest breach for us—between righteousness and unrighteousness, holiness and unholiness—he will connect even our burdened, unfaithful hearts to his heart of pure freedom and joy. I am overwhelmed by this promise and the effect it's had on my life: "He heals the brokenhearted and binds up their wounds."[1]

—

"I didn't think you had ever said a swear word before. But now I know you can swear without innocence."

My friend's words are said in humor, but they speak to the extremes I oscillated between only moments ago. It was in the last few minutes of a lengthy game of capture the flag, set in a densely wooded landscape hours after sunset. Someone had cheated. Not flagrantly, and yet, still enough to make me angry.

---

1 Psalms 147:3 ESV

There in the woods, surrounded by darkness and a dozen other college freshman, I barraged everyone and everything in sight with curses, insults, and animalistic screams. The game ended, and I transformed from a raging maniac back into my regular, kind self. My friends are understandably surprised.

Of course, I feel immensely guilty for my behavior. I scared myself with the sheer intensity of my sudden hatred. Every sane thought was crowded out by visions of violence. I had wanted to hurt someone—maybe even kill someone—over a game.

I know I've had similar outbursts before. I can remember scenarios when I lost my cool, along with my ever-beloved mind, not after an hour of growing frustration but in a single instant. These dots of red speckle my memory as far back as middle school. They stick out for their intensity and for their uncharacteristic nature.

I have been described, more times than I can count, as kind and patient. I have been in frustrating situations where everyone involved ended up losing their temper—everyone except me. I consider myself a forgiving person, and I try my best to overlook others' shortcomings. Most days this works so well for me. Ninety-nine percent of the time, I am a reasonable, self-controlled person. But then there are those moments. Without warning, I am unwarranted, incomprehensible rage.

More than a year passes, and I am playing another game. I'm an hour into a fun, competitive round of quidditch matches. Quidditch is a ridiculous game ripped from the fictional world of *Harry Potter*. In the books and movies, players fly around the sky riding magical brooms, throwing a ball through hoops to score points while avoiding a bunch of dangerous, magical flying dodgeballs. When translated into the non-fictional world, it's a ludicrous romp around a field while holding a broom, mop, or stick between your legs with one hand, a deflated soccer ball in the other hand, and getting pegged in the face with bean bags thrown by certain players. It's stupid, dangerous, and fun—meeting the only three qualifications needed to tempt college kids into trying it.

And in this glorious cacophony of chaos, I hold the highest honor. By the official fictional rules, quidditch matches do not end until one of the players catches the snitch. In the fantasy world, the snitch is a small golden orb with wings that flies randomly about the sky trying not to be caught by the only players, one from each team, that can snatch the snitch thereby ending the game. In the real world, the snitch is me—wearing a pair of running shoes and gym shorts, frantically racing on, off, and across the field of play, trying desperately to stay away from the two guys attempting to snag the gold ribbon attached to the back of my shorts.

As the current match drags on past the twelve minute mark, I take more risks—staying out on the field of play longer to ensure one of the seekers can catch me. With both at my heels, I frantically bob between players, cutting a lightning bolt scar from one end of the field to the other. I'm approaching the scoring hoops of the losing team, so I'm nearly to safety. If I can sprint past the hoops, I'll be off the field and out of range of the seekers, meaning I can breathe for a few seconds before it's time to turn around and retrace my path through the match. Only four strides left. Three strides. Two—

The keeper steps in front of me. I collide with him, smashing my face into his chest. Ricocheting off at an angle, I hit the ground hard on my side. The referee sounds his whistle. Bad form—no players besides the seekers are allowed to interact with the snitch.

I barely hear the whistle. Nor do I notice that the two guys who were chasing me a moment ago are now standing above me, asking if I'm okay, and offering to help me up. I'm still reeling from the impact, but I can feel my body filling with the white-hot heat of rage.

I hurl myself to my feet, screaming before I'm even standing. I curse and threaten the keeper. Or at least, I curse and threaten in his general direction. Anger and pain blurs my vision. I stagger about, unsure where the keeper walked off to. I pour out profanities and declarations of intended violence in enraged cries until every player and spectator stares.

My sanity slowly returns. I stop screaming. I walk off the field, carrying my burning desire to deck someone with me, before I'm ejected from both the game and the university. For a minute, I pace around in quick, violent strides. Then, the moment passes. The rage drains from my body. A fog of hate lifts from my mind.

"What am I doing?" I say to myself.

I realize with intense shame my unproportional response. The injury was minor. The pain from my crash has already subsided. I know the keeper; he's mild-mannered and kind. It was either an accident or he didn't know the rules to this obscure game—but he wasn't trying to hurt me. And why did I curse the people that happened to be standing around me? Where did all of this anger come from? I calculate there are a half dozen people I need to apologize to. Minutes after my outburst, I make my rounds of regret. The keeper apologizes to me with sincerity, and I feel even worse.

The next day, Sunday, the sermon delves into how past emotional hurts can affect our current way of thinking and behaving. With intensity, I'm reminded of yesterday's actions that I was trying to forget. For the rest of the day, I think back to the previous similar incidents. I never before thought that there was a reason behind my outbursts. Whenever they happened, I just told myself that I'd try to be nicer and more patient in the future. They were blue moon occurrences—easy to ignore because they didn't define who I was, most of the time anyway.

Now I meditate on them. I can identify some similarities between my enraged moments, between what set them off.

They seem to mostly occur during issues of fairness. And there is an intensely personal element about them. If I perceive some-one is taking advantage of me—hurting me—and I don't feel like recourse is available to me, then I very well may lose myself to hatred and a thirst for revenge.

I turn the mental puzzle to all sides, familiarizing myself with its surfaces, but I can't find the solution. Why? Why do I react in this way? What's the reason behind these uncontrollable moments? I ask God these questions. For the next few days, I pray, asking God to show me the reason, to give me the solution.

Less than a week after the quidditch game, I lie in bed half-asleep. I couldn't guess the time—perhaps eleven at night or maybe three in the morning. I'm vaguely aware of my room and my body. The bed lifts and falls like it's floating in the ocean. I don't know if I'm waking up or falling asleep. In my dreamy stu-por, I hear a voice speaking to me, but I can't focus on what it's saying. Then, a vision materializes in front of me. I see myself as a young boy, maybe five years old. The vision grows—it engulfs me. I'm no longer in my bed in my room but here in my own childhood, watching myself as a boy.

I see my younger self, and he is crying. I see my older brothers, and they are picking on him. He cries and grows angry. I can see in his desperate eyes how badly he wants to re-taliate. But his brothers are years older than him. He's too small and too dumb compared to them to do anything. He's helpless, and no one is there to defend him.

I can feel the promise his small, hurting heart is making. A promise that when he gets bigger, he won't let people treat him this way. He'll get back at them—he'll hurt them. It's an un-derstanding that no one is there to protect him—a decision to choose revenge and hatred over helplessness.

The vision wanes into darkness. I hear a voice speaking to me, and now I can make out the words clearly. I know it's the

Holy Spirit, and he asks me a question.

Do you want me to take this from you?

"Yes," I say. "Yes, I forgive my brothers."

I slip into nothingness.

I'm awakened by daylight pouring in from my windows. I sit up in my bed. I remember with surprise my vision in the night. Something feels different. I look around as if to find the source of an unknown sensation. I place a hand on my chest. My heart feels light. I laugh. I shake with spurts of giggles, unsure of why I'm even laughing. I get dressed, and my laughing continues. In me is an unshakable fortress of joy, and it blares its cannons and hoists its flags in jubilation. I smile through my morning routine. I prepare myself for one of the best days of my life.

———

The door for me to trust God's character was inner, emotional healing. As much as my brain believed that God was good, it didn't make much difference until my soul could say the same. When I first arrived at college, I thought I had a close relationship with God based on how often I prayed, read my Bible, and attended church. I had no idea the wounds in my heart kept me from trusting in God's character. And without trust, true intimacy is impossible.

Growing up in church, I heard talk of intimacy and closeness to God my entire life. But no matter how much I heard people preach on intimacy with God, and no matter how strongly I agreed with the messages, the concept of intimacy with God remained an aloof, ethereal reality. However, it all changed for me when God began to heal my heart from my past wounds. He prompted me to forgive others. He urged me to forgive myself—and even forgive him—for the greatest disappointments of my life. Intimacy moved from an abstract idea to an overwhelming experience.

It incepted when God became my dad, healing my deep sense of inadequacy that drove me to win love by performance. This healing transformed the way I interacted with God, allowing me to rest in his presence and consistently feel his love and delight in me. Eventually, this even led me to begin hearing from the Holy Spirit. After this came the way he healed the root of my anger issue, and many more emotional healings continued to take place.

To give you a sense of how varied the inner healings were, one area of healing worth mentioning regards racial bias. Growing up white around mostly white people, I always considered myself to be a saint in regards to race, meaning I never thought of someone as more than or less than depending on their skin color. In college, I began engaging in conversations about race with Jason—Jason is biracial, black and white—and other friends of different races. Thanks to my candid friends, I heard concerns and stories of injustice that were entirely foreign to me. And I must admit, it made me so uncomfortable, and I couldn't even tell why. So I began taking my discomfort to the Lord. Over time, through more conversations and the impressions of the Holy Spirit upon my heart, I became starkly aware of the fear and hatred that exists between different races and cultures, how that fear and hatred has shaped our societal systems in ways that oppress minorities, and how a portion of that fear and hatred was present in my own heart—even though it wasn't overtly evident by my actions. The Holy Spirit began pointing out subtle ways I was racially biased in my thinking and habits, and multiple times I was led to repentance. Through repentance I did not find guilt but relief, relief from a burden I was previously unaware of. I describe this process as healing because that's what it felt like in my mind and my heart. By removing my fear and hatred, God made room for love, love for people that look different than me with different backgrounds than me—people I may have simply ignored before. I have a long way to go to fully carry the heart Jesus has towards racial reconciliation, but I pray my life will mirror in some ways the prophecy of heaven—all nations, peoples, and tongues worshipping the Lord in unity.[2]

Following each emotional healing, the closeness of God's Spirit, the intensity of his love, increased in my life. Again and again, God broke my concept of intimacy by being more intimate with me than I ever thought was possible.

I have a friend who once illustrated well to me the stark difference between holding intimacy with God as a concept and experiencing it as reality. Macoby was one of my roommates in the rented house I lived in during the last year and half of college. He was passionate about growing in intimacy with the Holy Spirit. He was so passionate, in fact, that for a time he acted as though the Holy Spirit was a physical person who was always present with him. Whenever he drove a car, he would buckle the seat next to him because that was where the Holy Spirit was sitting. When he went for walks by himself, he would hold the Holy Spirit's hand. If he ate at a restaurant by himself, he asked for a table for two. And in his room next to his bed, he placed a chair for the Holy Spirit to sit in and sing over him each night that he slept.[3]

Some might consider his behavior to be weird or unbalanced, but Macoby cared more about increasing his awareness of God's physical presence than he cared about looking normal. And because of where he placed his priorities, he received a more complete reality of intimacy with God. The evidence of this can be seen in the fruit of Macoby's life. Macoby has seen more people miraculously healed by God's power when he prayed for them than anyone I personally know. This includes the opening of a blind eye—something I had the privilege of

---

2 Revelation 7:9-10
3 Zephaniah 3:17

witnessing. Not long after moving out of the rented house, Macoby started a successful business by following the leading of the Holy Spirit. He did so without a college degree and in a field he had no experience in. His success was entirely dependent on hearing from the Holy Spirit.

In juxtaposition, I've met a lot of normal and well-balanced Christians who would never do anything that could be considered strange or unorthodox in their pursuit of God. But many of these Christians have also never seen someone healed in an instant when they prayed for them. Many can't hear clearly from the Holy Spirit to be able to follow specific instructions for how to start or build an organization. And saddest of all, many of them struggle with knowing whether God is close to them or if they have even received salvation.

Once, while I was working at the virtual reality arcade, a man my age asked me if I had received salvation through Jesus. He and his friends had just finished playing a round of virtual reality video games, and while I was wiping down their headsets and controllers, he boldly popped the question.

"Yes, I have!" I told him, happy to run into a believer while at work. But he was persistent; he wanted to make sure I was in fact truly saved.

"That's great," he said. "But how do you know that you have been saved?"

"Well." I thought for a moment and answered with the first thing that came to mind. "Jesus said you will know his followers by their fruit. I know I belong to Jesus because of the fruit in my life, how my life has changed since I came to know Jesus."

With this answer he was satisfied and ceased to press the point. But after he left, I thought about the question for a greater length of time. I was reminded of when I was a young child, when I would pray to receive salvation several times a year because I was afraid that I still hadn't been saved for real. What changed? What allowed me to have so much confidence in my salvation that I hadn't questioned it for years?

At that moment, I realized the true reason I knew I had salvation in Jesus Christ. It was because the Holy Spirit told me that I did. Not once, but every day. God healed my heart and was bringing an increasing supply of his presence into my body on a regular basis. I knew God was my dad because he talked to me like a dad and was physically affectionate to me like a dad. I knew I was full of the Holy Spirit because he hung out with me like a friend and guided me like a mentor. I knew Jesus was my groom because he pursued me the way a man in love pursues a woman, and his romantic love melted my heart.

I don't want to shame anyone who struggles with whether they have received salvation or not. However, I do believe it is possible for anyone to enter into a relationship with God that's so deep and loving that fear associated with eternity—and any kind of fear for that matter—is entirely quashed. Not only is it possible but God is actively inviting each of us into such a relationship. There may be roadblocks, like I've mentioned before, such as incorrect thoughts, beliefs, and feelings about God and the way that he views us. But if we are willing to earnestly seek God, asking him to define himself for us, and take an honest look at our thought patterns and our past hurts that puts distance between us and him, then God helps us to remove those roadblocks.

Remember, God already took care of everything on his end when Jesus sacrificed his life for us on the cross. He desires to receive us, and he paid the price for sin with his own blood so he could. If there's an issue with us coming into an intimate relationship with God, it's on our end, not his.

For he desires to receive us as we are. But for our relationship with him to deepen, we have to allow him to transform us into the person he had in mind when he first thought to create us. Because only as that person, our true self, will we have the freedom to fully receive God's love and to fully give our love to him. It's impossible to give someone your whole heart when your heart is not whole. And the truth is, if we have not been renewed by the Holy Spirit, then our hearts are not whole.

Sometime after God healed me of my anger, I experienced an entirely unexpected reunion of my heart. On New Year's Eve, I drove to my parent's home with my youngest sister. We spent most of the evening with one of our brothers and his family, and we arrived back home late, a little before midnight.

Unready for the night to end, we sat in my room to continue our conversation from the car ride about God and our experiences with him. Then with a slow, gentle voice, like one searching for the kindest method to deliver a painful truth, my sister told me that the Holy Spirit recently spoke to her concerning our family.

"You know how our parents fought so much while we were growing up?" she asked. "Well, he showed me that each of the sons were affected by that in a different way."

Starting with the oldest, she explained how my brothers and I handled the hurt from our parents. For one it was humor—using jokes and laughter to help alleviate the pain of our family's brokenness. For another it was empathy—an absorption and deep feeling of the pain. And last on the list was me.

"The Holy Spirit told me that you've tried to be the family's savior. You see yourself as the knight in shining armor, and all of the pressure has been on you to come through."

Immediately I felt the depth of those words. Without ever conceiving them before, I knew them to be true in an instant. They acted as a legend for the map of my life. Suddenly, the puzzling marks and dashes became clear.

Beyond trying to earn love and significance from others, I had been motivated by the need to save my own family from brokeness for most of my life. And I did this by trying to become perfect. If I could look like a hero, be a glistening star of excellence that others admired, then my family would somehow be okay. I compensated for my family's dysfunction by increasing my own production. I needed to be the solution to any problem I encountered, because then the problem that affected me the most—the one I wished to resolve as a young child—could be solved as well. These unconscious beliefs originated in my wound, and they determined my path with invisible nudges.

I softly cried. My sister leaned into me, praying close to my ear. She prayed for me to release this burden, and she prayed for my heart to be made new. And as she prayed, the Holy Spirit spoke to me.

Your family already has a Savior. You don't have to save them; give them to me. Let them go. I am healing and saving your family. You don't have to walk around with a broken heart anymore. I have made you whole—the wound is healed, for real this time. Your wife will not be afraid of you. Your kids will not be afraid of you.

As God spoke the last two sentences in my mind, I wept openly. My sister hugged me tightly. Unconsciously, I was afraid; I had always been afraid of having a family of my own. I didn't want my future spouse or kids to be scared of me—scared of my anger and pain rising up from old, festering wounds.

In the same moment, the resolution came. In my chest swirled a whirlwind of sensation. I can only describe it as it felt: a piece of my heart, one that had been missing for most of my life, slid through my chest cavity and connected to the rest of it—like the final piece finishing a jigsaw puzzle.

As I cried, joyfully marveling over the beautiful weight of my whole and healed heart—my sister rejoicing with me—I heard fireworks, a long way off, exploding in deep, reverberating pops and booms, ushering in the beginning of a new year.

I do not pretend to be an expert on the subject of inner healing or deliverance. But there is one thing I have learned in my short number of years. Everyone, regardless of how free they appear or even believe themselves to be, carries burdens that God does not intend for them to carry. It may be unforgiveness towards others, towards themselves, or towards God. It may be deep, emotional wounds. It may be unhealthy expectations. It may be demonic influence—something I'll touch on in the next chapter—or any other number of things. There are in existence many helpful and healthy practices that help to alleviate these burdens. Psychological experts, self-care habits, and something as simple as physical exercise may help to reduce the effects these burdens have on people's lives. But most burdens, if not all burdens, have spiritual implications. And as such, we can never be fully free from them without an act of God.

And in that regard, we are fortunate. The heart of the Father is liberty. He longs to set us free of all burdens. There is only one burden he places on us, and that is his own love—a burden so light, at times it seems to be lifting me, so my toes barely scrape the ground as I walk.[4]

For anyone longing for liberty from burdens, my practical advice is this. First, connect with believers who are freer in God, freer in who God's made them to be, than you are—specifically those who are open about the burdens that God has freed them from and the hurts God has healed them from; that way you know they've gone through the process and aren't just faking it. God designed us to be in healthy community with others. Besides the encouraging words and advice that these believers can give you—which have been essential in my process—learning to trust others and being a part of a worshiping community is in itself a step in the direction of healing.

Second, be patient—both with God and with yourself. With God, because you won't fully understand the process he takes you through for healing and liberty. With yourself, because if past hurts start to surface, your first instinct will be to

---

4 Matthew 11:28-30

shove them down and tell yourself you've already moved passed them. It's easy to get frustrated with yourself when your weaknesses start to be exposed. Yet have biblical patience, not complacency. Don't lazily wait for God to act. God's heart is moved by petition—as is illustrated multiple times in the parables of Jesus. Be patient and constant in your pursuit of God and in your asking of him to make you whole.

As God continues to heal my heart, my trust in him grows. As my trust grows, one image, beautifully portrayed throughout the Bible, even more accurately describes the intimacy I have with God. Marriage. I belong to God, and he belongs to me. He is not far off. He is as close to me as possible—we are joined together as one. And because of our union, I am aware of his presence as strongly as I am aware of my own physical body. My heart turns giddy, my stomach sick, when I am alone with him. I feel his pleasure with intensity, in my emotions, in my soul, and in my body.

It wasn't hyperbole when Jesus called the Church his bride. Marriage is the clearest image of the union God wants with us. Too much of the Church works for God strictly out of duty. We have yet to understand that it is from love and enjoyment that a married couple gives birth to children. And it is in a house of love and joy that healthy children are raised. Lovely children are the fruit of a lovely marriage. And our union with God also produces fruit—from a place of love and enjoyment of one another. The fruit is varied as children are unique. Although for some people it is gifts, ministries, businesses, and creative acts of worship. And that Godly fruit will grow up to bless nations and bring salvation to many.

Those moments of intimacy, where the true fruit of my life is conceived, are difficult to describe because of their intensity and otherworldliness. There is nothing normal, safe, or religious about them. In those moments, God stops being everywhere and he starts being HERE. I become the ark of the covenant of old, full of the manifest presence of THE ONE, ALL POW-ERFUL, LIVING GOD. And after each encounter with him, another flame of his love burns within me. Each will burn for the rest of eternity.

If the Church wants to live with God in true intimacy, we must shed every layer of our religiosity and preconceived expectations of who and how God is. Only then will we be a blessing to all the earth. For too long we have carried the messages of God without carrying his presence. For too long we have sought to show others love without seeking to be one with Love himself.

The Church desires truth, and it seeks to preach truth. But often we forget that Truth is a person. We have only beheld absolute Truth when we have beheld Christ in intimacy. Jesus' words to the Pharisees still ring true for us as the modern Church:

"You search the Scriptures because you think that in them you have eternal life; and it is they that bear witness about me."[5]

How do I preach Jesus to a Church who believes they already know him? I ask this not in pride, for I know that I do not yet know Jesus myself—not nearly in the depth of knowing for which he longs from me. But I ask so you know the burning desire of my heart. For within this question lies one of the core purposes of my life: how can I urge others to reach higher? How can I spur on my brothers and sisters to reach out, even if in darkness, to feel their way towards God?[6]

Oh please, beloved Church, read these words that flow from my spirit like the tears that even now flow from my eyes. Please, reach higher. For the sake of the world and your very own hearts, leave the valley of religion and climb the holy mountain to meet face to face with God.

---

5 John 5:39 ESV
6 Acts 17:26-28

Out of this intimacy is birthed the passion and the power for our commission from Jesus—the same passion and power many churches ban and teach against.

"Go into all the world and proclaim the gospel to the whole creation. Whoever believes and is baptized will be saved, but whoever does not believe will be condemned. AND THESE SIGNS WILL ACCOMPANY THOSE WHO BELIEVE: in my name they will cast out demons; they will speak in new tongues; they will pick up serpents with their hands; and if they drink any deadly poison, it will not hurt them; they will lay their hands on the sick, and they will recover."[7]

How many churches would ban Jesus today from speaking from their pulpits, crying out, "That's not for today! Signs and wonders have ceased!" They want his parables but scorn his presence; they desire his teachings but are offended by his power. They mistakenly believe they can tame the Lion of the tribe of Judah. As such, they have built many zoos for people to attend. In droves people visit, hoping to catch a glimpse of the Lion. But the Lion isn't there. For if he was, his signs would follow, and the people would tremble at his might.

Intimacy that births power is what the Church is missing. We want to serve God so we seek training and qualifications. We get ordained to be a pastor or minister. Then we start programs and churches, thinking we are fulfilling the call of God. But God calls us into intimacy. In intimacy he qualifies us by making us like him—perfect and whole—the very righteousness of God.[8] In intimacy he gives us callings and purposes for our lives. In intimacy he baptizes us with fire to go and accomplish with the Holy Spirit whatever we've been given to do. Intimacy beats organizations, established churches, seminaries, and nonprofits. It trumps them all in effectiveness and reach.

Intimacy is the first step for the Church to be the light

---

7 Mark 16:15-18 ESV (emphasis added)
8 2 Corinthians 5:20-21

and salt of the earth. Only by believers choosing to sacrifice all in their pursuit of God will the Lord's Prayer come to pass—heaven coming down to earth.

For the rest of this book, I hope to show a glimpse of what it can look like when the kingdom of God is established on earth. For the rest of my life, I hope to be a part of its continual expansion.

Chapter 5

In which I begin to burn.

The virtual reality arcade was a nonstop, carousel of hilarious disaster. A select few brave young adults and I were charged with keeping the entire store from careening into utter destruction. Any shopping mall pedestrians looking for free entertainment could simply sit inside the bright, open shop to witness a cavalcade of dangerous activity.

First, they would see a man trying the plank walk. With headset on, the man was immersed in an animated world—one where he stood not on the floor of a shopping mall but instead on a plank of wood sticking off of the side of a building one hundred stories in the air. A small audience giggled, watching him nervously shuffle across the real plank of wood which happened to be sitting safely on solid ground. After repeating "This is so freaky! I actually feel like I'm really high in the air!" a few dozen times, he finally reached the very edge of both the real and virtual plank.

"You're at the edge. Now step off the plank and onto the ground. The floor is right in front of you, so all you have to do is put a foot out and set it on the floor to get off the plank," I instructed the man, as I was trained to do.

"Okay!" he said, beginning to sweat. The TV screen on the

wall next to him showed his view from his headset. He stood a thousand feet in the air, staring down at a busy city street below. "Okay, here I go!"

With a stiffened body, straight as the board he stood on, the man leaned forward, both of his feet planted firmly on the plank and his arms glued to his sides. He fell like a tree. The headset protruding from his skull dulled some of the impact as he smashed into the hard tile floor face-first. On the viewing screen, his virtual body fell to its virtual death.

My heart dropped into my stomach. Shaking, I hurried to the grounded skydiver and stood over his body looking for vital signs. He rolled over onto his back and pulled the headset off of his head.

"Dude! That was so realistic! Can I try it again?"

Walking farther into the store, a casual peruser would next come upon the virtual race car simulator. Here they watched customers take turns sitting in a car seat—complete with steering wheel, pedals, and a headset—that transported play-ers to a dirt road in some forest of Eastern Europe. Here they watched customers take turns sliding the virtual car chaotically down the rustic race track, crashing it full-speed into trees or launching it off a bump and into a ditch every ten seconds. And here they watched customers take turns yanking off their headset—overcome by motion sickness—and wobble around dizzy holding their stomach after just a few minutes of driving. Lucky perusers could even catch the occasional expulsion of food court wares into the small trash can conveniently placed next to the driver's seat.

Lastly, all store visitors could watch with glee the death-defying main event of our mad circus. Farther into the store were the virtual reality rooms. These eight by eight feet constructions consisted of three walls and a small couch where the fourth wall should have been. Inside the rooms, customers played a variety of video games by putting on a headset and picking up two plastic sticks that operated as controllers. They were then transported to a digital world where the controllers they held acted as their hands. If they wanted to pick up a rock or a gun or a sword or a book or any other item to interact with, all they had to do was walk over to it, reach out a controller, and squeeze the button their trigger finger rested on. In this way, customers explored strange worlds, battled monsters, and repaired cars—all within a tiny room while their friends watched from the couch.

The setup was fun, awe-inspiring, and catastrophic. Everything you can imagine going wrong went wrong nearly every time a person put on their headset. First, there were the walls. The players couldn't see the walls, of course, because they were wearing headsets showing an open world around them. While playing games, if they happened to get too close to one of the walls, the headset would display small blue lines, like a wall of laser beams, showing them exactly where their physical boundaries were. Though, actively playing intense video games as they were, it was very difficult for the players to pay attention to the boundaries. Every few minutes, someone would punch a wall, walk into a wall, run into a wall, or even scream, jump away from a virtual monster, and bounce off of a wall. To make matters worse, one of these walls wasn't a wall at all but a couch hosting naive, unexpecting friends. As such, I often witnessed gamers, wielding a virtual sword and shield, hack and slash their loved ones with real plastic batons.

Falls were common. People tripped over their own feet since feet weren't displayed in the games. Self-injury abounded. People smacked themselves in the face with their own controllers. They nearly hanged themselves as they got tangled up with the cords that ran off the headsets. But somehow, the days always ended without customers threatening to sue. And for that, I always felt like I was witnessing a miracle.

Recently, after a lengthy conversation with my mom about the kingdom of God, my time at the virtual reality arcade suddenly became a useful analogy for me to understand the physical and spiritual reality we humans find ourselves in. We must understand that the physical world is nothing more than a virtual projection within a truer, spiritual reality. Like the players putting on their headsets, we are stepping into a limited and fixed world when we are born. Through our senses, we perceive only what is within this physical world. This world is dynamic and real enough that many believe there to be no higher reality.

But the moment a player believes that what he sees in his headset and hears through his headphones is all that exists—forgetting about the greater outside world—then it stops being a game and starts being a prison. Without an awareness of the true world around him, he will begin to trip over his own feet and bump into walls, unable to understand why he is being hurt. After some time, his true body will become hungry and thirsty. He may find virtual sustenance within the game, but no matter how much he gorges himself, his true body will never be satisfied.

This is a picture of what it is like to live within a physical reality while surrounded by the spiritual. God created everything both seen and unseen. We were created with a body, but it is our spirit that will live beyond even the stars. And with our spirit, we perceive the spirit world. With our spirit, we perceive the greatest reality of the kingdom of light. With our spirit, we perceive the worse reality of the kingdom of darkness.

To journey further into God's kingdom is to embrace this spiritual reality. Every person, alive or dead, lives either in God's kingdom or the kingdom of Satan. The lives of everyone on this planet are greatly affected by which kingdom their truest bodies, their spirits, find themselves in—the realm of life or the realm of death. The physical world is shaped, of course, by physical means. However, it is also influenced greatly by the spiritual forces of both heaven and hell, of both love and hate. Unbelievers who deny this live in ignorance. Christians who deny this, whether outright or by their practical choices, live in a delusion.

It is a hard thing, at least it is for me, to consistently be aware of the spiritual reality we live in. One reason for this, I believe, is the fear of turning into a raving, super-spiritual basket case who nobody can relate to.

In American Christian culture, we often preach and live the gospel of balance. We believe there's a happy medium to everything, and that it's best not to be extreme or radical about anything. "Overly spiritual" individuals make us uncomfortable, angry even, because they offend the balance that we hold so dear. Unfortunately, the path of being Jesus' disciple is not one of balance. It is one of godly wisdom, humility, gentleness, and also of fire, but rarely of balance. Our emphasis on living a balanced life, void of extremes, is really just an avenue for us to spread out our hope across several areas. We place our hope in ourselves or our family but not all of our hope. We place our hope in our career or in financial opportunities but not all of it because we know that would be unbalanced. And after depositing hope in many different places, we transfer all that is left of our hope to the person of Jesus.

Laying every ounce of our hope on God feels unbalanced—not to mention insanely risky. But the throne of our hearts were made for God to sit on. We can't allow any other concern to share that seat. Jesus said that whoever loves his life will lose it, and only by giving up your life will you find any at all.[1] But don't fall into the church trap—believing that giving your whole life to God means giving up every passion you have in order to work full-time in a traditional ministry context, preferably doing something that you hate since that builds character. Instead, understand that God made you and your passion uniquely, and he wants to direct your life uniquely.

---

1 Luke 9:24

All other sources we can place our hope in, anything we attempt to draw life from—even ourselves—are empty wells. Full hope in God equals a full life. He is the only thing our hearts were designed to fully hope in, and therefore, he alone will not disappoint.

I need life. I need to live the true reality—not a lie. I cannot afford to hope in anything else besides him. When people ask me what I'm hoping for—what I'm counting on, what the plan for my life is, what my imagined future is—I want my answer to be, "My God is the one who raises the dead." I can't afford a backup plan.

For most of this book, I have written with the hope to bring godly freedom to Christians. I have circled around three themes: God's will is not paralyzing but liberating, intimacy with Jesus is everything, and the importance of seeking the Holy Spirit for emotional and spiritual healing as well as the correction of deeply held beliefs. In this last chapter, I want to reach beyond these themes to give examples of what the Church can look like when it steps out of lies and traps and begins to walk in freedom toward the center of God's kingdom.

However, before I get there, I have to write a little bit about love. I believe one of the reasons the Church can put an unhealthy form of pressure on fellow Christians to work hard and do great things for the Lord is because, in general, we have a weak grasp of the Father's love. And yet, we deeply believe that we are supposed to be making an impact and changing lives for Christ. That leaves us amping ourselves up to start churches, create nonprofit organizations, write books, record new worship songs, or obtain a Master's of Divinity. None of these things are evil, far from it. But if we believe that in them is the power to change the world or even one person's heart, we will miss what God wants to do on the earth.

Before we do anything as a Christian, we must receive a

revelation of the Father's love. When we are better at receiving the Father's love, we are better at loving others. Transferring the Father's love to those around us is our ultimate destiny on the earth. The reason this doesn't seem like enough is because we have already tried the whole love thing. "Love your neighbor" does not sound world-changing because it brings up pictures of saying nice stuff and holding open the door for people. Those actions are kind, but even worldly people can do them. There is nothing transformative about loving others in our human ability. If we try to be generous, caring people, then we will do a lot of good—but good is all we will ever do. God will not be able to use us to flip society upside down.

It is my firm belief that an ounce of God's true love can change the course of a person's life in a moment. The reason we as the Church are so inadequate in the heart changing business is because we are simply poor receivers of God's love. We eat up the crackers and olives off of God's dinner table, thinking that will sustain us and our ministry, and then we head out and try to serve God and others. I believe God's calling us back into the dining room, to sit down, and to enjoy the feast he has prepared for us.

The thing about true love is it comes entirely from God. You cannot fabricate it. You can't trick people into thinking you have it when you don't. You can't make up for a lack of it by compensating with biblical knowledge or ministry training. This is why uneducated people can do more for the kingdom and receive a greater reward in heaven than people with degrees and worldly influence to shape ministries, businesses, and society. We are all on an equal playing field when it comes to God. The things that give us advantages and opportunities in the physical world do not aid us in the kingdom. God is searching for the ones who can receive and carry his love. Those are who he chooses to use.

Say you lived in a tiny village of fifty people. If you received a deep outpouring of the Father's love and were obedient in loving your village the way God stirred in you to do with the love he gave you, your life could have more eternal significance than a megachurch pastor who preached incredible biblical messages to thousands of people and gave ninety percent of his income to the poor for his entire life. Don't believe me? Why don't you ask Apostle Paul:

"If I speak in the tongues of men and of angels, but have not love, I am a noisy gong or a clanging cymbal. And if I have prophetic powers, and understand all mysteries and all knowledge, and if I have all faith, so as to remove mountains, but have not love, I am nothing. If I give away all I have, and if I deliver up my body to be burned, but have not love, I gain nothing."[2]

I have heard it said that love is an action, not a feeling. There is an element of truth in that, but there is also room for a grave misunderstanding of love in that saying. You can see in what Paul wrote that it is possible to perform many "loving" actions without possessing an ounce of true love. True love comes from the Lord, and it is both light and substance. We cannot be a light if there is no light in us. We cannot offer a substance to others that we have not first received ourselves. When God's love fills us, it manifests as action and feeling; truth and power; wisdom and abandonment; freedom and selflessness.

We as the Church desire to be a beacon of hope for the lost of this world. Yet the truth is, if we are not focused on receiving the Father's love inside of ourselves, we are wasting the world's time. We won't have anything to give that could truly save them and bring them freedom.

I say all this as a warning: don't let this chapter stir you up to perform more for God apart from his love. Instead, let it encourage you to continue laying the foundation of true intima-

---

2 1 Corinthians 13:1-3 ESV

cy with God in your life. That way you can partner with God to impact others in the way he's designed you to work with him.

———

It's two in the morning. Someone is knocking on my bedroom door. The taps are quiet, yet firm—only a couple decibels too loud to ignore by turning back over in my sleep. A thought floats around in my groggy mind. "Nothing good happens after two a.m." I must have heard that years ago, back in high school. It was something that my friend's parents would say. I guess it meant they wanted their kids home soon after midnight.

"Hello," I mutter. Please, God, let no one answer. Let it be my imagination so I can drift off again.

The door cracks open, enough for a face to insert itself into my room.

"Hey, Reese, could you come out into the hallway? I need you and Macoby's help."

My housemate, Ian, slides his face out of my room and closes the door. Now I can hear him knocking on Macoby's door. With a deep sigh of reluctance, I throw back my sheets and blankets and sit up in my bed.

I've rented a house with some friends for nearly a year. Together, we've had our share of excitement, both good and bad. But no one in the house brings as much excitement to the living quarters as Ian. This mainly stems from the kind of people he brings over to the house. Ian loves God, and he has a deep desire to help others. Sometimes, I just wish he would give us a little more heads-up before he starts helping another person, because we often are enlisted to help by proximity. The tally of homeless friends that Ian has invited to stay in our living room at different times stands at four. I have a sneaking suspicion that this wakeup call will involve us helping him help someone else.

I stumble into the hallway, yawning. Ian's flipped the hallway light switch. Macoby's out of bed, too, looking as tired as I am. With a calm voice, void of any tone of emergency, Ian gives his explanation.

"Thanks for getting up. Here's the thing. I have my friend Jordan over. We've been staying up talking in my room. He's been dealing with a lot of stuff lately and he's struggling with drugs, so I wanted to pray for him. But when I tried praying for him, he started manifesting and jumped off the couch and hit his head on the ground. He's still manifesting, so I need you guys to come help me pray for him so he will calm down."

And with that he turns around and walks away. The hallway is silent. Macoby and I look at each other. In his face, I think I can read something along the lines of, "Please tell me this is a joke," and I know it mirrors my own expression.

I've been running with the charismatic crowd long enough now to know what Ian means by "manifesting." However, I have to ask Macoby anyway, out of sheer disbelief of what is currently happening.

"When he says 'manifesting'—does he mean, like, a demon?"

"Yeah. I guess so," Macoby answers dully.

I look down the hall. I slide my eyes back over to give Macoby a second hesitant glance. Without another word, we creep slowly through the living room, through the kitchen, and out the side door leading into the garage.

Ian's room is a refurbished garage. And by "refurbished" I mean a regular garage stuffed with rugs, bookshelves, a couch, a mattress, and a collection of bikes leaning against the large metal door. Ian was kind enough to volunteer to live in the garage when we decided to fit four people in a small, three bedroom house. I push aside the hanging blanket serving as a bedroom door and step down onto the hard concrete floor.

I see Jordan. He is seated in an almost fetal position on the couch. His body convulses with constant, unnerving twitches. There is something strange in his eyes. They dart around for a few moments, then suddenly stare fixed in front of him, then dart around again—I get the sense that they aren't seeing much of anything. I see blood. A small amount drips from a gash on the side of his head, presumably from when he leapt off the coach like a madman after Ian began a simple prayer. I hear a strange mumbling noise. Jordan's mouth quivers open and close, letting out a constant babble of incoherent sounds. Ian stands beside him. Macoby and I take a step closer. Not for a moment does Jordan acknowledge our presence.

Ian looks at us expectantly. Now I can catch a small glimpse of worry in his eyes.

"Okay!" he says. "Let's start praying!"

And we do. Out loud, all three of us pray. We thank Jesus for his blood and his work on the cross. We invite the Holy Spirit to come and meet with us in this sketchy garage. We command the evil spirit to be bound up and to stop affecting Jordan. We pray for just a couple minutes, and a change occurs.

Jordan's twitches slow down. He starts to breathe a little more regularly and stops mumbling as often. He lets himself sink into a slightly more comfortable position. He still looks out of his mind, but at least it's an improvement.

The three of us come closer. I sit on the floor in front of Jordan. Macoby, Ian, and I take turns engaging him, asking him different questions to get a sense of where he is. He answers sparingly. We tell him that he is experiencing demonic oppression. We tell him that Jesus wants to set him free.

"You don't understand," he says. He doesn't look at us when he speaks, though his eyes flinch in our direction. Conversing with him feels like trying to talk to a man who is submerged underwater.

We pray over him again. He settles down even more. We ask him more questions, and he starts to answer us a little more clearly. I feel like we are getting through to him with our message of hope in Jesus. Then suddenly, Macoby asks me if I will lead him through forgiveness.

"Okay," I say, unsure exactly of what I just agreed to. Maybe because of how tired I am, maybe because of the Holy Spirit, but I find myself saying words to Jordan without even thinking about them.

"The most common door that the enemy uses to attack us is unforgiveness," I tell Jordan. "We can hold unforgiveness towards others for the way they've hurt us, towards ourselves because of our mistakes or because we don't think we are good enough, and towards God because we usually blame him when anything bad happens in our lives. But unforgiveness is an open door that allows demons to attack us. I'm going to lead you in some prayers to forgive others, yourself, and God. First, I feel like you need to forgive your dad."

Amazingly, Jordan follows along, genuinely repeating my prayers of forgiveness. He forgives several people, he forgives himself, and finally, he forgives God for how hard his life has been. When he reaches the end, he lets out a long sigh of relief. He looks at us. For the first time since stepping into the garage, I see a fully conscious person in front of me.

We talk with him a little longer. We pray with him to receive Jesus and the Holy Spirit, and he does so willingly. He thanks us. He stands up, completely sane, looking in every way unlike before. The dried blood on the side of his head is the only trace left of the episode.

Having begun only thirty minutes ago, the excitement ends and Macoby and I stumble back to our beds. As I drift off to sleep, the same thought echoes again and again in my mind.

"Well, that was incredibly easy. All we did was pray, and the demon left. God's so much bigger than Satan and all of his demons. God's so much bigger. He's so much bigger."

Intimacy with God is not like intimacy among people. Intimacy with others can make us feel loved and appreciated, or even giddy and romantic. With humans, there isn't much beyond this. Of course, there is value in intimate friendships; there is value in the loving intimacy of marriage. The world, and too often we as the Church, simply attribute more value to human relationships than they warrant.

The best way to explain what I mean can be found in a single word: adventure. I believe everyone craves adventure. No one wants to merely live. We want excitement; we want purpose and meaning. We want our hearts to beat for more than simply survival. Only those crushed by others and circumstances seem to lack all desire for adventure. But a wick for adventure lies in the heart of every man, woman, and child. At any moment, it can catch aflame. I don't mean every person is secretly an adrenaline junky. You can desire to live your life to the fullest without having any desire to go skydiving. Our hearts are unique. Our personal adventures are also unique, and they can often be unappreciated by others.

Among my generation, which is young at present, the desire for adventure abounds. Corporate marketing directors understand this. If you want to sell us youngsters something, all you need to do is hype up two words around the product: authentic and adventure. Authenticity feeds into adventure. We want our adventures to be the real thing, not plastic and contrived.

Older generations too desire adventure. A word I've heard often said by those further down the road than me is legacy. Legacy is simply adventure for the mature. They want their life to have counted for something. They want to look back and see the battles they've won that will make a difference even when they've passed.

This brings me back to intimacy. Many people believe that

the adventure their heart desires can be found in another person. All of them are setting themselves up for disappointment and disillusionment. Connecting to another person doesn't change who we are. It doesn't propel us into a nonstop, exciting adventure. It doesn't provide a deep, lasting sense of meaning. The world thinks it does, though. That's why most popular songs are love songs. That's why our culture worships sex like it's the be all and end all.

Intimacy with God is not like intimacy with people. Intimacy with God means adventure. If we're bored with Christianity, we're hanging around too many Christians and not enough God. He propels us into circumstances we never would walk into willingly on our own. He draws our spirit into endless realms of purpose and beauty. Any moment I choose to follow Jesus with my entire being, I'm instantly swept up in the grandest story ever told. I don't even have to leave the house.

No one pushes us into a life of adventure and meaning more than the Holy Spirit. And no one asks us to risk more. Risky is not a word often used to describe the Church. Loving, welcoming, and caring are words many of our churches hope to fulfill. But if you want to know what it looks like for the Church to step into its true destiny, to live in the very heart of God's kingdom, it looks like risk.

Paul once described the kingdom of God as righteousness, peace, and joy in the Holy Spirit, and rightly so.[3] The Church desires these attributes, and we often declare to the world that we possess them. Yet, so often it's a farce. The Church in general does not abound in the righteousness of God, peace that surpasses understanding, nor joy that can fill a man with strength. It's like, as Christians, we are taught to live in denial. We too often portray a level of goodness to the world that's not actually present in our lives.

---

3 Romans 14:17

We forget what Jesus once said about the kingdom of God:

"From the days of John the Baptist until now the kingdom of heaven has suffered violence, and the violent take it by force."[4]

The Church wants the spoils without the battle. We can display trophies that belong to prizefighters when we've never thrown a punch, or taken a hit, in our lives.

Remember how the earliest Church stepped into their righteousness, peace, and joy? After being filled with the fire of the Holy Spirit, Peter stood up and boldly defied the current culture and religious environment by preaching Jesus, the Son of God, resurrected. Thousands came to Christ and began to meet together daily—worshiping God, devoting themselves to the teaching of the apostles and to the fellowship of believers, and sharing all that they had. Then the persecution began, and they were imprisoned, killed, and scattered. And yet, they continued to preach Jesus to the ends of the earth. The members of the earliest Church knew what it meant to fight for something. They knew how to risk all for Jesus. If we desire righteousness, peace, and joy in the Holy Spirit, we must be ready for the violence that accompanies grasping the kingdom of heaven. We can be safe or we can be the Lord's bride—we can't have it both ways.

One way to understand "taking the kingdom by force" is by analyzing the tension Christians experience between what is promised to us and what is our present reality. I see this playing out in my life often. Anytime that I feel like the Lord is inviting me into something new and exciting with him, or anytime that I receive a prophetic word about something God wants to do in my life, it's like I suddenly have a door to new possibilities in front of me. Although Jesus has already paid the price for me to step into the future God has for me, I still have to decide to open that door. But sometimes, I pull on the handle and the door doesn't budge. It's jammed. It won't swing effortlessly open.

---

4 Matthew 11:12 ESV

At this point, I could hang my head and walk away sad, thinking that I must have heard God wrong. Or, I can tug on that door, day after day, until it finally swings wide open.

Seeking God's kingdom looks like prayer and obedience. It looks like pressing into God for the gifts that he has promised. Paul wouldn't have told us to "earnestly desire the greater gifts"[5] if we were just going to automatically receive them anyway. Then what would be the point of desiring them?

I remember the night I began to desire the greater gifts of God. My sophomore year of college, my church grew enough to develop a young adult small group. One autumn night, Caleb, Macoby, a handful of other friends, and I hit up a street festival in OKC's Midtown district. After placing our orders with some on demand poets, we decided to check out the live music.

A single DJ manned a fleet of keyboards and looping devices, crafting techno music for a small energetic crowd. Naturally we jumped in and created our own dance circle. A guy my age was dancing near us. He was good, so we quickly pulled him into our circle. The girl he was with stood close by and watched.

After a while, the music mellowed out, and we started talking to the young man and his girlfriend. The man talked at length about his love of dancing. This soon led him to start bemoaning the pain and weakness of one of his ankles. He used to be able to land a standing backflip, he told us. Then he and his girlfriend got in a car wreck, about a year ago, and his ankle hadn't fully healed. His girlfriend chimed in to tell us about the screws that were surgically placed into her shoulder after the wreck, and about how much they hurt whenever it's cold outside. They were hurting her now, she said.

Macoby responded first, asking if we can pray for them. We started with the dancer's ankle. We prayed, and he tested it

---

5 1 Corinthians 12:31 NASB

out. It wasn't hurting anymore, he told us. But he really wanted to put it to the test. Right in front of us, he performed a standing backflip.

"It's healed! It doesn't hurt at all!" he said almost yelling.

Then we asked the girl if we could pray for her. She was reluctant; neither of them were believers. But her boyfriend was adamant, telling her that he was healed and that she needed to let us pray for her. So she let us. We prayed for her, and she moved her arm around, trying to initiate the pain she was so used to feeling in her shoulder. It too was gone.

We were ecstatic. This was the first time our small group had done something like this together. We took the couple to a nearby coffee shop and talked with them some more about their lives and about the love of Jesus.

That night lit a fire in me to experience a greater spiritual reality. From then on, anytime I heard Christians talk about failing church attendance or the difficulty of appearing relevant to a post-truth society, I would think back to that night. I knew that the physical healing piqued that couple's interest in Jesus. Before that moment, God was just a lifeless idea that some people they knew believed in. The healing was God's love being made real and tangible for them.

I was beginning to experience a small amount of the gifts and power available to us through the Holy Spirit. And anytime I brought this kind of thing up around ninety percent of my Christian friends, I would receive the same responses: "That's not for everybody," "God just hasn't gifted me in that way," and "God may heal some people, but most of the time it just isn't his will." Yet, I knew that the young couple weren't healed just because it happened to be God's will. They were healed because people in our small group had been seeking God for the gift of healing. I knew that Macoby had diligently prayed for many people to be healed—for a year—before he saw anyone affected by his prayers. And all around me I saw Christians who occasionally asked God to heal someone, but who never risked looking stupid to actually see someone healed. I began to feel like the Church was hamstringing itself.

Almost a year later, as I grew in my ability to hear from the Holy Spirit, I felt God pushing me to pursue the gift of supernatural healing through Jesus. A new semester began. I told myself that I was going to pray for every sick or injured person I saw, whether I knew them or not.

The first day of the semester began strong. A friend of mine on the women's soccer team was complaining about her leg—she had pulled a muscle during practice. It wasn't a major injury, but it hurt when she walked on it. She let me pray for her. I asked her to test it out. With genuine surprise, she moved her leg around and stood on it, trying to activate the pain. Jesus healed her. The injury was completely gone. I spent the rest of the night praising God.

That experience hyped me up. I was sure the rest of the semester was going to be just like that. God was going to heal dozens of people through me. I thought the sports coaches would start asking me to come to games just to pray over injured players. So I kept praying. Anyone I saw with a noticeable injury or sickness, any person who mentioned feeling sickly or in pain, I prayed for all of them. For about two weeks.

No one else was healed. Not one. I got discouraged, so I took a little break and only prayed for people sparingly. But after a couple more weeks, I felt the Holy Spirit stirring up my heart to continue. Coming out of a stellar church service, I was motivated enough to start back up the next day. I prayed diligently for a couple more weeks, asking about a dozen people if I could pray for them. No one was healed. Not one felt an ounce better. I quit my pursuit. Soon, however, I felt the Holy Spirit stirring up in me, again, the desire to see others healed.

Thus, a wheel of motivation and discouragement rolled over and over through the semester. Despite the weeks I spent passionately praying for healing—sandwiched between weeks spent wallowing in defeat—the end of the semester drew near and not a single person more had supernaturally recovered. Daily, I would watch the same injured athletes hopping down the hallway on crutches. Each one had allowed me to pray for them on multiple occasions. Their casts and braces mocked my efforts and solidified my defeat. Then I understood something. I had once wondered how strange it is that a large portion of the American Church genuinely believes that God still heals people today. I thought this was strange because, I wondered, if many of us do in fact believe that God heals today, then how come all of us aren't constantly praying for people to be healed? Isn't the best way to see people get healed for us to pray for as many people as we can? Seeing my friends on crutches, I understood why we don't. It's because it sucks. It sucks to pray for people, fully believing they will be healed, only to see nothing happen.

As the semester closed, I felt the Holy Spirit trying to stir up my heart to continue praying for people during the next semester. It was time for me to have an honest conversation with God.

"I don't want to do this anymore," I told him. "I've been praying for people all semester. Besides that one person at the beginning, no one else has been healed or even felt a tiny bit better."

The Holy Spirit spoke in my mind.

Why does that make you want to stop praying for people?

"Because it's disappointing," I responded. "I get myself hyped up to pray for people only to get let down again and again when no one is healed."

Why do you get disappointed?

"Because they didn't get healed. I want to see people healed, so it's disappointing when nothing happens."

No. Why do YOU get disappointed when someone isn't healed?

The question struck my mind, and I was forced to reflect.

Suddenly, I had an insight into what was truly causing my cycle of emotional highs and lows all semester.

"It's because it makes me feel like a failure. If someone isn't healed, I think it's my fault. I think I could have done better somehow. I could have prayed harder or believed more."

But you can't heal anyone. I'm the God who heals, not you. You should never feel disappointed in yourself for something that you have no power to do.

His words addressed a subtle error in my thinking. I knew that God wanted to use me to heal others. However, I also believed that I possessed some ability to make healing happen through force of will or well-spoken prayers. That was my fallacy.

The Holy Spirit's words shifted my mindset about not only healing but all spiritual gifts. The truth is, God alone can heal, prophesy, or perform any supernatural work. The Lord chooses to impart his work through his children. I get to be a part of this. But there is a price to pay: I have to die to myself. I can't carry an ounce of pride or fear. If being used by God boosts my own ego, then I'll be shattered whenever someone isn't healed or my prophetic words fall completely flat. If I'm afraid of looking silly or strange, then I won't step out and take a risk when I feel the Holy Spirit leading me.

God has revealed to me his burning passion to partner with me, and all other believers, to do impossible, supernatural works on the earth. But he has also shown me how my own insecurity limits what he can do. How is that so? Because God displays his glory through his kids. But my own insecurity wants to hold on to a measure of false glory for myself. I want to be liked and respected. I want to feel like a winner, not a loser. The hard truth is that risking everything to partner with God can look a lot like failing. God often invites us down roads that initially bear no external fruit. But if we choose to partner with him, the end results are always incredible.

The reason we see such little supernatural activity in

America is because very few believers are willing to walk that difficult road to reach the results. Perseverance is what's needed. It's so easy for us to discount ourselves or to discount God after trying and failing at something a handful of times.

I can't write any further without addressing faith. Along my road of partnering with the Holy Spirit, I've been forced to grapple with the issue of faith as it relates to the supernatural work of God. After much laboring over the concept, I have discovered what I believe to be a very profound truth: faith is the most annoying part of Christianity.

I'm kidding—mostly. Although, let me explain why I've genuinely had the thought, "Man, this whole faith thing kind of stinks."

When I think about how the Church talks about faith, especially as it regards seeing God perform some kind of supernatural work for us or for others, I believe much of the discussion to be unhelpful and even harmful. Faith is largely viewed as some kind of magical substance. Good Christians have a lot of it; bad Christians have very little. You need a lot of this faith-stuff for God to heal you, bless you, or deliver you. As such, if God has not healed you, blessed you, or delivered you in a certain way, that is concrete evidence that you possess a shockingly small amount of the magical sparkly substance known as faith. But how do you acquire more of this powerful faith-stuff you ask? Well, the answer is simple. All you need to do to have more faith is this: just have more faith. That's right. Just produce it spontaneously somehow. Is that not working out for you? Then try thinking really, really hard that whatever you are asking God for is definitely going to happen. Maybe you can conjure up more faith by sheer willpower. I don't know—your guess is as good as mine.

One summer, I worked as a camp counselor at an outdoor Christian camp. One of my fellow counselors was almost deaf, but he could hear through the use of hearing aids. After we had become friends, I felt the Holy Spirit nudging me to ask him if I can pray for his hearing. My friend was happy to let me pray for him, and I prayed for his hearing to be restored and also for him to experience more of the love of God. (Regardless of whether someone is healed or not, I always want every person I pray for to leave that interaction feeling loved by God.) No change occurred in his hearing, but he thanked me for praying for him. Then he told me something.

"A lot of people have prayed for my ears to be healed. My uncle told me that the reason I'm not healed is because I don't have enough faith."

His words and expression pained me. We'd been friends long enough for me to know that he deeply loved Jesus. Here was a believer genuinely following after God, even sharing the truth of the gospel with others, and yet another believer's words were making him feel inadequate.

"That's not right," I said. "Faith is just trust in God. You do trust God; you're trusting in Jesus for your salvation. You trust God enough to follow him and obey him. Your deafness isn't a sign of a lack of faith. A lot of people choose not to follow God because they are sick or something bad has happened to them; they think it's God's fault or it's proof that he doesn't exist. The fact that you've chosen to follow God, despite not having perfect health, is proof that you trust God."

He'd never viewed his faith in that way, and the thought was liberating to him. I could see a measure of condemnation lift off of his shoulders. Just as I should never judge myself for not healing someone when I pray for them, no one should judge themselves for not being healed when others pray for them.

This world is messy. Earlier in this book I wrote about the complexity of the different wills at work around us—God's will, Satan's will, and the will of fallen man. So many Christians judge their measure of faith, or others, by whether or not they live in good health, good finances, and good circumstances. They forget that this world is fallen and sin-ridden, and that affects us all. We can have all the faith in the world, but each of our bodies will still get weak and die someday. We can't completely insulate ourselves from the troubles of the world no matter how hard we trust in the Lord. The Bible confirms this in the book of James:

"Count it all joy, my brothers, when you meet trials of various kinds, for you know that the testing of your faith produces steadfastness. And let steadfastness have its full effect, that you may be perfect and complete, lacking in nothing."[6]

Notice that James does not say, "When you meet trials of various kinds, that means that you do not have enough faith." He also does not say, "When you meet trails of various kinds, that means that God has purposely caused all of those bad things in your life to happen, including you getting sick and your loved one dying, because that's his mysterious way of turning you into a better Christian." Instead, he says to count it all joy, because hardships cause us to fortify our faith with steadfastness. The fire of difficulties refines the metal of our faith. And when we continue to trust in God, in spite of hardships, we will be made perfect and complete in him. Comfort is not the goal—dependance on God is.

Think about that for a minute. We spend so much effort trying to become more capable and independent. We think that self-improvement is the door to happiness and fulfillment. The world even praises people who have the most achievements or money or good looks like they are demigods. However, the message of the gospel is that we can't and God can. We can't save ourselves; God can. We can't renew ourselves; God can. We can't heal or deliver or provide for ourselves; God can. We can't create a life full of meaning, but God can give us his life in place of ours. When we try our hardest to be capable and independent,

---

6 James 1:2-4 ESV

the world gives us temporary trinkets as our reward. When we swallow our pride and depend on God, he gives us himself as our reward. This is why dependance on God is the goal. If we can shed our need to feel capable and independent—if we can learn to fully depend on God in this life—then it's like we're living with a foot already in heaven.

Personally, I believe it is much more useful to view faith as trust in God than as a magical substance. That's because faith is not about the one who believes but the one who is believed in. Jesus is the object of our faith. I can try to play mental games when I pray, focusing intently on what I want to happen, believing that I'm increasing my faith. Or, I can let my trust in Jesus grow organically as I get to know him better. No one can fully trust a stranger. No one can fully trust someone whose motives and intentions are hidden. As I've grown in intimacy with Jesus, as I've allowed him to reveal himself to me, my trust in him has naturally grown. I trust him as my healer because I've seen the desire to heal in his heart. I trust him as my provider because he's shared with me his intent to provide for me.

Even when we feel disconnected from God, we can still see his perfect will in the person of Jesus in the gospels. Jesus said he only did what he saw the Father doing.[7] And what did he do? Heal, deliver, and save. We can read the works of Jesus and have confidence that his will for today has not changed.

I know that there are people who are sick or in trouble who have prayed or been prayed for a hundred times and have yet to see a solution. But I also know that the will of God is to heal, deliver, and save. And if more Christians constantly prayed for others with that truth in mind, choosing to depend on God rather than giving up prematurely, then the Church would see greater numbers healed, delivered, and saved. Lack of steadfastness is keeping us from becoming perfect and complete.

---

7 John 5:19

God commissioned us to be ambassadors of the kingdom of God. The same way that Jesus demonstrated the kingdom, we are to demonstrate the kingdom. We are to be coheirs to the authority and fulfilled promises that Jesus won on the cross.[8] We are to receive the true, abundant life that Jesus promised us.[9] Yet, it's so easy for us to give up on this grand adventure. We let hardships and feelings of inadequacy defeat us. We let controversies around faith, God's will, and the gifts of the Spirit rob us from stepping into our destiny as the Church. Instead, we must learn to face these challenges and questions by running directly into God's arms. Let's let difficulties and doubt fuel our dependence on God. And as we continue to follow Jesus with our whole hearts, we will fulfill this charge:

"And as you go, preach this message: 'Heaven's kingdom realm is accessible, close enough to touch.' You must continually bring healing to lepers and to those who are sick, and make it your habit to break off the demonic presence from people, and raise the dead back to life. Freely you have received the power of the kingdom, so freely release it to others."[10]

Although I get discouraged at times, I've continued to follow the leading of the Holy Spirit. As such, I've been privileged to experience incredible things in God. Physical healing is just a part of it—though, it's one of my favorites.

At my church, we often ask the Lord for words of knowledge during pre-service prayer. Words of knowledge are insights into how people around us need to be ministered to. One such morning, sometime after my semester spent praying for people with no results, I heard God telling me that someone coming to church that day had knee pain. I shared this with those at pre-service prayer. Several others also shared words

---

8 Romans 8:16-17 and Matthew 28:18-20
9 John 10:10
10 Matthew 10:7-8 TPT

of knowledge concerning pain and sickness. Later, towards the end of the service, our pastor Rachel shared all the words of knowledge with the whole church, and almost a dozen people responded by coming up to the front to be prayed for. I went up as well, with many others, to pray for healing.

I walked up to a group of three people who had gathered around Rachel for prayer. All three of them had severe pain in one of their knees. Rachel began praying over them. As I prayed quietly to myself, I heard the Holy Spirit tell me to touch each of the hurting knees, one by one. I did so as I was praying. When Rachel finished praying, all three told us the pain was completely gone. One lady told me that the moment I touched her knee, all the pain left. Each of them tested out their knees with squats and jumps, and they couldn't feel any pain or weakness. The oldest of the group went into a deep squat, laid down with his back to the ground, and then rolled forward and stood up again, something he could not do before we prayed for him.

Many at my church are constantly praying for God to manifest his kingdom with signs and miracles. As such, we get to see people healed both physically and emotionally, as well as delivered from demonic oppression. We've witnessed countless healings from pain and injury. I've watched people jump up and down while weeping because their long-standing leg injuries were healed. I've seen people lift their arms straight up—overjoyed because moments before they couldn't lift their arms to eye level. I've seen a blind eye opened. I've seen a lady healed of triple vision, her eyesight instantly normalized.

A couple in our church unsuccessfully tried to have a child for two years. The wife had a condition that made it difficult to become pregnant. One night, a visiting minister prayed for the couple at our church. Two months later, the wife discovered she was pregnant. Unfortunately, the baby was born prematurely and with a genetic abnormality. After her birth, our whole church began to pray for the child. After more tests, the doctors were surprised to find that the genetic abnormality they iden-tified at her birth had somehow disappeared. Today, she is a young healthy child.

Another time, Rachel was experiencing so much lower back pain that she didn't think she'd be able to go on a trip that she and Grant had planned for the next day. Several of us gath-ered around her to pray. A man named Joseph heard the Holy Spirit tell him that one of Rachel's legs was shorter than the other. He asked her if this was the case. Rachel sat down and put out both her legs to see. All of us stared in amazement. Her left leg was a few inches shorter than the right. Her hips and back were so twisted up that it was causing the difference. Without ever touching her feet or legs, Joseph prayed over Rachel, and we all stood around in a circle and agreed with the prayer. Suddenly, Rachel's left leg moved, as if it was growing in length, and matched the length of the other. We collectively gasped in shock. She stood up, and her back pain was significantly de-creased. She regained her mobility in an instant—only feeling soreness instead of intense chronic pain. She went on the trip, and over a few days even the soreness left.

A quick note: I know that there are individuals out there who fabricate the "leg growing" healing I described above by literally pulling people's legs (an ironic statement if there ever was one). Unfortunately, such shameless shenanigans can hurt the testimony of real miraculous healings. The true work of the Holy Spirit will always stand apart from those who use decep-tion to impress others.

I tell these stories to honor the God who performs mira-cles to this day. I tell them as evidence that the kingdom of God is at hand. His kingdom is limitless. Far greater miracles than what I've seen are demonstrated regularly throughout the global Church. If we seek his kingdom without ceasing, the glory and power of God will be seen in our churches, in our homes, in our streets, in our places of business, and in all of society.

A reason so many Christians spend their lives on the outskirts of God's kingdom is because they have grown accustomed to a certain kind of Christianity, whatever it may be, and they prefer that Christianity over the Christianity demonstrated in the Bible through the lives of Jesus, the disciples, and the earliest Church members. Many have rejected the Holy Spirit—his ministry and his gifts—simply because he doesn't fit within the man-made boundaries of the faith to which they adhere. By choosing to keep and protect what they currently possess, they lose out on the new thing that God wants to do in their lives. They miss out on a greater—an experiential—revelation of God.

There are questions I want to ask the Church. Is God our father, or is he not? Is Jesus our friend and husband, or is he not? Are we filled with the Holy Spirit, or are we not? We say yes so often to these questions, yet if the answer is truly yes, it should change everything. We need to stop acting like orphans and embrace the Father's love. We need to stop living alone and embrace intimacy with Jesus. We need to stop playing it safe and embrace a life of risk and power through the Holy Spirit.

The purpose of this book is not to be a doctrinal creed. I am not trying to define the truest expression of Christianity; I do not believe that to even be possible. God made each of us uniquely, and we are meant to connect to God and experience him uniquely. What each of us do have in common—that which is the essential element to our faith—is that no man comes to the Father except through Jesus Christ.[11] As Christians, we have the tendency to approach God through the lens of our past religious experience and our denominational teachings, not through the living person of Jesus alone.

My prayer is that we would be like the Samaritans of that certain town. They believed in Jesus because the woman at the well told them about him and her experience with him. But they

---

11 John 14:6

soon no longer relied on the woman's testimony because they sought out Jesus to experience him for themselves.

"They said to her, 'It is no longer because of what you said that we believe, for we have heard ourselves, and we know that this is indeed the Savior of the world.'"[12]

My conviction is that more of us need to hear and know Christ for ourselves. My evidence that there is a lack of this in the Church can be found in the gospel of Matthew, when John the Baptist prophesied what Jesus would do when he came to his people.

"I baptize you with water for repentance, but he who is coming after me is mightier than I, whose sandals I am not worthy to carry. He will baptize you with the Holy Spirit and fire."[13]

Many Christians have accepted the baptism of John but rejected the baptism of Jesus. We've repented of our sins to be baptized with water, but have we truly accepted all of Jesus—including his fiery baptism?

Apostle Paul understood the importance of the baptism of Jesus. When Paul meets followers of Christ who are not walking in the power of the Holy Spirit, this is how their interaction plays out:

"And he said to them, 'Did you receive the Holy Spirit when you believed?' And they said, 'No, we have not even heard that there is a Holy Spirit.' And he said, 'Into what then were you baptized?' They said, 'Into John's baptism.' And Paul said, 'John baptized with the baptism of repentance, telling the people to believe in the one who was to come after him, that is, Jesus.' On hearing this, they were baptized in the name of the Lord Jesus. And when Paul had laid his hands on them, the Holy Spirit came on them, and they began speaking in tongues and prophesying."[14]

---

12 John 4:42 ESV
13 Matthew 3:11 ESV
14 Acts 19:1-6 ESV

As Christians, it's easy for us to live like we "have not even heard that there is a Holy Spirit"—that is, without any ounce of God's power. That's because we've been trained to separate Jesus from his baptism of fire. We can believe in repentance and salvation, we can esteem Jesus' teachings, but if we are not taking seriously Jesus' promise of the Holy Spirit, we are rejecting the baptism of Jesus Christ.

There are other Christians who have asked Jesus for the Holy Spirit, and they believe that they now experience all of the Spirit that Jesus desires to pour out on them. But the words of Jesus found in Luke 11:5-13 challenge that notion. Jesus tells a couple of parables to encourage his disciples to ask and continue asking the Father for good gifts. He ends the teaching by declaring:

"If you then, who are evil, know how to give good gifts to your children, how much more will the heavenly Father give the Holy Spirit to those who ask him!"

We may have asked the Father, through Jesus, for the Holy Spirit at one time, but have we continued to ask and seek him to intimately know more of his Spirit?

The belief that we currently have all the power, the presence, and the giftings that God wants to give us cripples us from expanding our impact. I've heard countless Christians tell me, "I can't do (fill in the blank). That's just not an area I'm gifted in," as well as, "I can't heal, I can't pray in the Spirit, and I can't prophecy; those just aren't gifts God's given me." My only answer is this: neither could the members of the early Church do any of those things until they were baptized with fire.

Before Jesus ascended, he told his disciples not to do anything until they received the Holy Spirit. And then they prayed together for ten days—waiting for and expecting the Holy Spirit to come. They were rewarded with a dramatic baptism in the fire of God. And they still didn't have all of God's Spirit that Jesus desired to pour out on them. Later in Acts, the Spirit fell on them again in another dramatic fashion.[15] In juxtaposition, today Christians pray for two minutes to receive the Holy Spirit. Then after that one time event, they believe that they must have it all. "If God wanted me to have more power or more gifts," they think, "he would have given it to me. But this is all I am meant to have."

Whether we have rejected the ministry of the Holy Spirit or have ceased asking to experience more of him, the evidence that the Church lacks fire is clear. Simply put, I don't feel heat radiating off of most Christians. We are cold, lifeless, and ineffective. If the majority of Christians were baptized with the Holy Spirit and fire through Jesus Christ, the Church would be burning. And the hurting and lost would come to warm themselves by the fire.

Each step I take into God's kingdom is simply a deeper embrace of my identity in Christ. First, I am the Father's son. In this identity, I receive acceptance and validation from the Father. Next, I am the bride of Christ. Here I'm invited into deep intimacy and friendship with Jesus. And now, I am the temple of the Living God.

Under the old covenant, God's Spirit hung out almost exclusively in the ark of the covenant. This majestic box literally housed God. As such, his presence filled the room the ark rested in with tangible glory—the Holy of Holies of the Hebrew tabernacle and temple. Under the new covenant, God doesn't hang out in a box or temple anymore. He lives in you. Every Christian is a temple of God's Spirit.[16] The Church, as a collection of people, is the new ark of the covenant, housing the Holy Spirit on earth.

"I am a temple of God" is something I've said since children's church. But the notion held little weight for most of my life. More recently though, God's urged me to accept this

---

15 Acts 4:32
16 1 Corinthians 3:16

incomprehensible truth with the whole of my being. Today, it rattles me. It's impossible; it makes absolutely no sense. It scares me. Yet, it's true. My very body is home to the creator of the universe.

What does this mean for us? How are we to live, knowing that God himself lives inside of us? To say it in a single word: worship. The Hebrew temple was a place of worship and sacrifice to God. The children of Israel would bring their offerings to the temple at appointed times, and then they would return to their homes. As the modern Church, we confuse our role with that of the children of Israel. We are not to bring offerings of worship to God, only at appointed times, and then return to our normal lives. We are not like the worshippers of old. We are the temple itself.

For us, worship is not an action but part of our identity. Just as the temple was made to house God and be a place of continual worship, so we were made with this purpose in mind. At all times, we can position ourselves to worship God in reverence as his presence constantly fills us. This is why Paul says, "Whatever you do, do all to the glory of God."[17] Worship isn't a part-time job or a spiritual discipline to be performed on Sundays. It's who we are as temples. God's Spirit abides with us each passing moment. The cry of our hearts, through all that we do, should be offerings of honor and gratitude and adoration to him.

As I wrote before, we can't experience the new life God's calling us into if we aren't open to letting go of our old notions of what Christianity is—and even who we are. My advice: ask the Holy Spirit to make you a temple of God, and always be open to new things from him. My warning: crazy stuff might happen.

Around the time God started urging me to accept my iden-

---

17 1 Corinthians 10:31 ESV

tity as his temple, one of these crazy things happened to me. A minister named Timothy Berry visited my church for a weekend. For three days, he taught extensively on the Holy Spirit and his gifts. On the last night, Timothy and his team prayed for every person in the church, one at a time. When Timothy got to me, he prayed that I would be filled with more of the Holy Spirit. I should note that at this time, I was already filled with the Holy Spirit and saw gifts operating in my life—such as the gift of healing and of praying in tongues.

In a few moments, Timothy moved on to pray for the next person. I continued to stand, palms up, focused on receiving anything God wanted to give me. After a couple more minutes, my body felt heavy. I laid down on the floor because it was more comfortable than standing. Then it happened. Slowly, beginning at my head and then moving to my feet, my entire body started vibrating. It felt like each of my cells were bursting with energy. When I closed my eyes, I pictured myself engulfed in fire— flames leaping off of me. I shook. Minor convulsions engaged my core, lifting my head off the ground. I rocked side to side. My fingers curled, making claw-like fists, and I crossed my arms over my chest. Many times, with effort, I unfurled my fingers and lay my arms at my sides, but the moment I stopped forcing my arms into that position, my fingers would curl and my arms would cross back over each other on my chest. I could not stop the constant trembling in my body with any effort.

My shaking episode lasted around twenty minutes. That was the first; it's occurred four more times since then. Three were during church meetings. One happened during my personal prayer time—lying down on my bedroom floor.

Talk of these experiences spooks some Christians. Still others seek after intense, spiritual moments such as these like religious adrenaline junkies. But I don't write about this experience to tell others to pursue such phenomena. I write to say what Jesus did in my spirit during those moments. Each time

I finally stood up, my spirit felt refreshed and empowered. He secured my identity. He built up my faith in him. He gave clarity to my purpose. These things, and things I do not understand, took place in my spirit as my body and mind shook in confusion. There are many other ways the Lord has developed my spirit as well—ways that did not engage my physical body—but I would not be who I am today void of those times of intensity.

Many Christians limit how God can work in their lives because they reject anything that doesn't seem familiar and safe—anything they can't understand. We must realize that the ways in which we are comfortable with God speaking to us may not be the only ways God wants to speak to us. Dealings with God can often be uncomfortable, even unfathomable.

I'm not saying we should force any strange experiences to happen. Some people do that—using performance and frantic exuberance to compensate for lack of connection to God's Spirit. I hate that religiosity. I've seen way too many leaders physically push people over as they pray for them, causing people to "fall out" and lay on the ground as if God was the one who knocked them over. This sort of conduct gives the Church reason to judge real moves of the Holy Spirit as no more than performance and ridiculous behavior. Yet, I do not doubt the power and intensity of the Holy Spirit. When the Spirit falls like fire, there's no need for pushing and performance to make it look like something is happening. If you're open to receive, free from preconceived notions, anything can happen. You may find yourself on the floor. You may find yourself dancing. You may laugh. You may weep. You may do none of these things. But there is one way to know for certain it is the Holy Spirit. You will walk away changed.

Once, while shaking uncontrollably on the ground under the presence of the Holy Spirit, I had a short conversation with God. He opened by asking me a question.

How will you hold the fire?

"I don't know," I said aloud to him. The fire he referred to I could only imagine as being the power and presence of the Holy Spirit—the same fire causing my body to convulse. "How will I hold the fire?" I asked back.

With your whole life.

And I understood in that moment that the Holy Spirit isn't for Sundays and special occasions. If I want him, I have to let him spread into all of my life—the entirety of my being.

If we understand how fire works, then we understand in part how the kingdom of God works. Fire cannot remain burning forever on the same log. It spreads, or it dies. When God's kingdom catches fire in our hearts, it starts spreading within us until it consumes every part of us. But we can keep it from spreading. We can isolate the flame, compartmentalizing our lives in order to keep Jesus within acceptable boundaries. We can dig a fire pit, limiting the way the Holy Spirit can take shape. We can reject the kingdom's growth—"Sit in a corner and behave. Don't do anything weird, and don't show up anywhere you're not invited." But unless we're willing to embrace the engulfing flames in all areas of our lives, the fire is going to stop burning. However, when we let the Holy Spirit's renewing power redefine and recreate every facet of our identities, God's kingdom is established deep within us. Absent of this, the only thing established is a kingdom of religion.

The same is true of the Church. God's kingdom is expressed on earth through the Church. It's fire cannot remain only inside religious gatherings. We must spread it to each realm of society and culture—to every log—lest the fire run out of fuel.

What does it look like for the Church, living not in the shadows but in the center of the kingdom of God, to carry this fire? Essentially, it looks like the renewal of the entire world. It looks like Christians bringing the presence, wisdom, power, and love of God into every country, every government, every business, every expression of life. It looks like the fire of the kingdom burning up the sin-marred wreck of this world and leading all of culture into true life. It looks like God using his people to destroy the work of the enemy and to establish Jesus' holy rule over all things. Some of what I've talked about in this book are hints to how that can look specifically, but to be honest, I don't know the details of how that will be played out in your own life. That's something the Holy Spirit himself will have to reveal to you.

However, I can tell you how to ensure that you do your part to make it happen. And this is where I hope to cut out every measure of "try harder," "be a better Christian," and "do more for God" that may be construed from this book. Any attempt to establish God's kingdom in this world by our own efforts will completely fail. The answer, the answer to every question in fact, is to surrender yourself to Jesus. I'm not talking about a simple prayer of salvation—for what Christian has not prayed such a prayer? I'm talking about giving Jesus his due reward.

You may think that Jesus died for us just because he is a really nice God, but that's not the only reason. The Bible says that for the joy set before him Jesus endured the cross.[18] That means something motivated him. A future joy propelled him to bear all sin and sacrifice his life. That future joy—that's you. The Bible calls you the inheritance of God.[19] You are what he worked for. You are what he bet all of his chips on. You are what he died for. At the end of time, life will dissolve and all of history will resolve—and Jesus inheriting you will be what it was all for.

Let me make this clear. He paid for you with everything he had. He carried your sin and consequences. He was mocked, tortured, and killed for you. He took the blow of death aimed at you. We can't even begin to understand the magnitude of this—God choosing death so we can have life. So understand this: Jesus wants what he paid for. He wants his reward. He wants his

---

18 Hebrews 12:1-2
19 Ephesians 1:18 and Psalms 94:14

inheritance. All of it. He wants you. Not a part of you. Not most of you. He is a jealous God.[20] He wants you. All of you.

If this sounds too scary and intense, remember that the Bible tells us it is the goodness of God that leads us to repentance.[21] That means that God is so good, as we begin to understand him more clearly, our hearts will yearn to turn towards him more and more. If surrendering to Jesus puts you on edge, ask God to show you more of his goodness. All of the goodness of creation can be traced back to God. As you see more of this connection, you will naturally want him more.

Giving all of myself to Jesus is a road I walk every day. It's a spiritual path. It runs miles beneath the path of my physical life. What I do for work, where I go to school, who I marry, where I live, how I spend my money, how I spend my time—these things are only surface level, yet often they vie for my complete attention. Giving myself to Jesus occurs deeper—beneath the bedrock of my physical existence. It's difficult to describe; it is beyond language. In the innermost essence of myself, I give myself to Jesus. And somehow, there is always more to give.

What can I tell you but to give yourself to him? If I said, "pray this much," "read this much Scripture," "give this much money," or "go to church this much," I may be speaking only to your surface. I may give the false notion that through religious acts you can renew yourself and the world. The only "work" required under this new covenant is that of surrender—and it is a work that begins at our core.

We can trust Jesus to lead us down the spiritual road. We can trust him to liberate us, to heal us, to renew us, to empower us, and to equip us. Every ounce of true freedom and life is to be found along that path. But we can choose not to follow him down it. We can instead choose to better ourselves and the

---

20 Exodus 34:14
21 Romans 2:4

world through good works. However, the eternal impact won't be there. God can do more through you in a day, as a surrendered vessel who's walked the lengthy road to healing and renewal, than you could do in a thousand lifetimes on your own.

That's why the progression of intimacy and inner healing is so important for the Church to make its mark on this world. In the book of Genesis, Jacob experienced a powerful vision where he saw heaven opened and angels ascending and descending down and up a ladder.[22] He named that place Bethel—the house of God. Later, a house of God was literally constructed, first with the tabernacle, then with the first and second temple— places for heaven to be open above and for God to descend upon. Yet these constructions were mere archetypes, metaphors for a coming greater reality. That reality is us. We were made to be houses of God—ladders beneath open heavens. The measure to which God's kingdom can flow through us is directly linked to the state of our hearts and minds. We are meant to be open portals, but all of us have junk blocking the doorway somewhere. Where are we hurting from unhealed wounds? How are our thoughts keeping us from aligning with him? What walls have we put up? What fears are keeping us from him? How are we denying his love by our own self-judgement and self-hatred? The answers may not come immediately. Growing in knowing yourself, like growing in knowing God, is a process that takes a lifetime. When we pursue these processes as one, they become a pilgrimage worth taking.

I know the transformative fire of God is coming to the Western Church at large. I know the Holy Spirit is working to lead the global Church straight into the light of God's kingdom.

Recently, while driving home to OKC after visiting a family member in Arkansas, the Holy Spirit spoke to me about the fire

---

22 Genesis 28:10-19

I will get to see. Praying as I drove, suddenly, in the corner of my eye, I caught a glimpse of a massive grass fire off on the side of the road. I immediately turned my head to see this burning field. Nothing. There was no fire—just an empty field of grass. In bewilderment, I drove on, unsure how my eyes could play such a trick on me. Then my head started to tingle. The tingling increased until it felt like small tongues of fire where dancing about on top of my skull. I freaked.

"What the heck is happening!? God, is this you? What are you trying to tell me?" I said aloud.

I drove on. I waited on the Holy Spirit to speak to me, and I grew in anticipation as I heard nothing. Then I saw it. A large road sign proclaiming, "Welcome to Oklahoma!" stood down the road in front of me. I crossed the border. The moment I changed states, my heart exploded. I jumped in my seat, overcome with excitement; I didn't even know what I was excited about. For some unknown reason, I was almost too emotional to drive. Then the Holy Spirit spoke to me.

I'm bringing my fire to Oklahoma. I'm going to burn up the religious systems that produce zero fruit. I'm going to bring my life into every realm of the state.

As he spoke, I fully believed the reality that God's revival fire is coming to my home. I have never been more excited about anything in my entire life.

I believe God is doing a work to transform the face of Christianity and the Church as we know it—here in America and the entire Western world. No longer will we be a Church of pastors and churchgoers, quietly living out religious lives in our isolated bubbles. We will be a network of true sons and daughters of God, bringing fire and life-changing love to every realm of society we are connected to. We will be marked by intimacy with the Creator—carrying the level of authority, power, and wisdom that only comes through an authentic, face-to-face relationship with God.

I live in the Bible Belt—the very buckle of the Bible Belt as I see it. And God's spoken to me his desire to begin a transforming work here, in this part of the country, that will reverberate out to the entire Church. As an intercessor who regularly prays to see this work done in my lifetime, I want to encourage you to seek God for what he wants to do in your city, state, and region. Once you have a vision for what God is doing in your area, you can partner with God by praying it into existence. I believe that in unique ways, God desires to impart his fire upon every region of the earth, to see the earth transformed into an image of heaven.

But let's not confuse the fire of transformation with the fire of judgment. Too many Christians act just like the disciples did after a certain city rejected Jesus.

"When his disciples James and John saw this, they said, 'Lord, do you want us to command fire to come down from heaven and consume them?' But he turned and rebuked them, and said, 'You do not know what kind of spirit you are of; for the Son of Man did not come to destroy men's lives, but to save them.'"[23]

It's far too easy to sit back and cast judgment on the world. I do not pretend that judgement fire does not exist; Jesus talked often about the coming day of judgment. But that's God's job. It's not for us to dish out. I've met too many Christians who can talk for hours about how terrible a state the world is in, and how terrible a state other Christian denominations are in, but who can't talk for a few minutes about the good God is doing on the earth today.

We can't adopt a posture of negativity. We can't just wait around for Jesus to come back, feeling smug about our holiness while pointing out one another's flaws. If we do, we've doomed the world. But if we embrace the Lord's transformative fire, we've done our part to save it. Jesus brought the kingdom of God into

---

23 Luke 9:54-56 NASB

the world, and he passed that baton off to us. We are to bring the kingdom to every corner of life, until life itself runs out.

The beauty of this reality cannot be properly written. My aim for this book is to replicate a single stroke in a masterpiece painting. The Lord desires to display the fullness of this wonder in our hearts. In love, he leads us into his kingdom. Hand and hand with him, we enlarge the boundaries of his territory. His work always begins in intimacy, inside our union with him. Our spirits blossom under his hands. Our face reflects the glory of his own—our hands, extensions of his own. With burning passion, we lean into the vitality of his life. We step into the intensity of the purest story—a story we could never write on our own. Voices trembling, we cry out to him. For eternity, he's cried out to us. Our words unite in song:

> Arise, my darling!
> Come quickly, my beloved.
> Come and be the graceful gazelle with me.
> Come be like a dancing deer with me.
> We will dance in the high place of the sky,
> Yes, on the mountains of fragrant spice.
> Forever we shall be united as one![24]

---

24 Song of Solomon 8:14 TPT

THANK YOU

It means so much to me that you've read this book. If it blessed you, please leave it a review on Amazon.com or GoodReads.com.

If you want to keep up with what I'm doing, visit my blog (holdingfireblog.com), or follow me on Facebook and Instagram (@reeseblackholdingfire).

Godspeed,
Reese Black

Made in the USA
Monee, IL
12 January 2021